THE GOLDEN AGE OF

FLY-FISHING

THE GOLDEN AGE OF
FLY-FISHING

THE BEST OF
THE SPORTSMAN
1927–1937

Introduction by Ken Callahan

With Illustrations by A.L. Ripley and Ralph Boyer

RALF COYKENDALL, EDITOR

The Countryman Press

WOODSTOCK, VERMONT

Library of Congress Cataloging-in-Publication Data

The golden age of fly-fishing : the best of the Sportsman, 1927–1937 / edited by Ralf Coykendall ;
foreword by Ken Callahan ; with illustrations by A. L. Ripley and Ralph Boyer.

p.   cm.

ISBN 0-88150-398-3 (alk. paper)

1. Fly fishing.   I. Coykendall, Ralf W. (Ralf Wales), 1929–   . II. Sportsman.

SH456.G65   1997

799.1'24--dc21   97-10387

CIP

Text and cover design by Trina Stahl
Cover illustration by A.L. Ripley
Illustrations by A.L. Ripley, pages 12, 22, 25, 30, 33, 35, 37,
40, 45, 48, 52, 54, 55, 73, 74, 83, 87, 90, 101, 103, 105,
109, 110, 121, 122, 125, 143, 149, 154, 164, 170, 171
Illustrations by Ralph Boyer, pages 19, 51, 58, 63, 65, 77, 81,
85, 97, 117, 132, 145, 161, 167

Published by The Countryman Press
PO Box 748, Woodstock, Vermont 05091

Distributed by W. W. Norton & Company, Inc.
500 Fifth Avenue, New York, New York 10110
Printed in the United States of America
10 9 8 7 6 5 4 3 2 1

This is for my son, Chip,
and for Sam, Richard, Matt, and Russ,
who had the good sense to fall in love
with my daughters.

CONTENTS

———

FOREWORD

———

THE ALL-TOO-BRIEF span of twenty-odd years between the two great wars to end all wars was called the Golden Age of American Sport, and for good reason. It was a time of peace and plenty. Fish and game abounded; the automobile brought distant woods and waters within reach; and the nation's sportsmen and -women went afield in record numbers. Many fine writers chronicled those halcyon once-upon-a-time years, and I am pleased to bring you the best writers from the best magazine of those or any other times: *The Sportsman*.

If the 1920s and '30s were the golden age of sport, it must be stated that *The Sportsman* provided the jewels that made those years shine most brightly. In the thoughtful and thorough introduction that follows, Ken Callahan provides an overview and insights to this once-in-a-lifetime publication; my remarks about *The Sportsman* are therefore limited to—if you will forgive a bit of nostalgia—a few words from a boy who cut his teeth on that wonderful magazine.

I was only a gleam in my father's eye when the farsighted founders of *The Sportsman* tapped him to be the new magazine's advertising director prior to its January 1927 debut, and by the time I came along, late in 1929, the magazine was completing its second successful year. *The Sportsman* paid the finest sporting artists and writers top dollar for their contributions, and advertisers paid top dollar to climb aboard. It flourished de-spite the dust and Depression of the 1930s. Not until a little man with a small mustache and a large, evil ego changed the world did the publication fold its tent, and the golden age fade to an afterglow. Fortunately, the words and pictures of that once-upon-a-time remain glowing embers, and the boy who cut his teeth on *The Sportsman* is still around to rekindle the flames.

Fly-fishing has changed since the time of *The Sportsman,* and it hasn't changed at all. Newfangled materials and fluorescent flies may have replaced time-honored cane and natural hackles, but anglers still tempt trout and salmon with tiny bits of fluff using techniques that were perfected during the golden age of fly-fishing and reported in *The Sportsman.* This collection is therefore more than informative and enjoyable; it is a link to our angling heritage, and the boy I was is pleased to bring it to a new generation.

— RALF COYKENDALL
Manchester Center, Vermont

INTRODUCTION

P UBLISHED BY wealthy men for their wealthy readers, *The Sportsman* ran from the height of the financial boom of the 1920s through the dark years of the Depression. The tone and content of the magazine didn't change over the years, even during the Depression. It was aimed at the sportsmen and -women who had the money and leisure to pursue their hobbies, their sports, and their social lives during good times and bad.

I know of no more pleasurable way to lose an entire day than to dip into old copies of *The Sportsman*. I pick up an issue to look at one article and find myself absorbed by all of the others: by the etchings and paintings of Benson, Ripley, Schaldach, Bishop, and Pleissner; even by the advertisements (Rolls-Royces, motorboats, single malt Scotches were all repre-

sented). No matter what your sporting interest—speedboats, horse shows, polo, ballooning, golf, tennis, dog shows, mountain climbing, rowing, college football, the Olympics, foxhunting—you'll read about it here. And that is in addition to *The Sportsman*'s fine articles on fishing. I have never come across a magazine with a more varied selection of articles on such interesting subjects.

Still, the magazine is certainly one of the best-kept secrets in modern sporting literature. In November 1937 it merged with *Country Life*, and its identity was lost. Many collectors and booksellers today have never even heard of it—I only discovered it about ten years ago. Complete sets of the magazine are rare. With their large format (10¼ by 13½ inches, roughly the size of *Life* magazine), all 128 issues take up a lot of space on the shelf. Their scarcity is also due in part to the high original selling price (fifty cents per issue!) and the limited number of subscription sales. Many of the magazines, too, have been cut up by collectors and dealers for the illustrated ads.

Certain issues are especially valuable. The September 1933 issue, for example, contains Ernest Gee's twenty-eight-page bound-in checklist of early sport books, itself a useful and sought-after reference. My own set also includes three loose supplements that were issued with the magazines: "Fox Hunting Formalities" by J. Stanley Reeve, "African Game Lands" by Prentiss N. Gray, and a very large fold-out chart of "Open Seasons For Game 1929–30." All of these supplements are even scarcer than the magazines, and collectible in their own right.

Trying to assemble a complete set, issue by issue, is an expensive and frustrating exercise. Buying a complete set is also expensive—but if you're lucky enough to find one, you won't spend the rest of your life trying to track down the elusive loose issues. If you get the chance to buy a set, grab it while you can—they aren't offered for sale very often, especially not as bound sets.

———

Everything about *The Sportsman* was impressive: the design, the ads, the interesting mix of subjects, the artwork—and, of course, the writing, from the finest sporting authors of the time. Ralf Coykendall's selection of angling articles for this anthology will give you a taste of the good things hidden away in this paragon of American sporting periodicals.

— KEN CALLAHAN
Sharon, New Hampshire

THE SPORTSMAN'S CHARTER

THIS MAGAZINE was founded and is published by a group of amateur sportsmen who have dedicated it to these convictions:

That sport is something done for the fun of doing it and that it ceases to be sport when it becomes a business, something done for what there is in it;

That amateurism is something of the heart and spirit—not a matter of exact technical qualifications;

That the good manners of sport are fundamentally important;

That the code must be strictly upheld;

That the whole structure of sport is not only preserved from the absurdity of undue importance, but is justified by a kind of romance which animates it, and by the positive virtues of courage, patience, good temper, and unselfishness which are demanded by the code;

That the exploitation of sport for profit kills the spirit and retains only the husk and semblance of the thing;

That the qualities of frankness, courage, and sincerity which mark the good sportsman in private life shall mark all discussions of his interests in this publication.

FREDERICK WHITE is best known for his early Derrydale Press book *The Spicklefisherman and Others,* published in 1928. I have no doubt that Eugene Connett, who served as a consultant to *The Sportsman,* was responsible for his appearance in that fine publication on the eve of the 1929 trout fishing season.

THE FISH THAT GET AWAY

THEY ARE THE UNDISCOVERED STARS IN
EVERY GOOD ANGLER'S HEAVEN

———

by FREDERICK WHITE

YEARS AGO, Willard Spencer, composer, librettist, and a famous trout fisherman of his day, wrote a song, entitled: "The Biggest Fish I Ever Caught Was the One That Got Away." Undoubtedly, the title of the song and its subject matter were induced by the persistent mental picture of one of those harrowing experiences which every angler, no matter how skillful, undergoes and which, in retrospect, frequently bulk larger in the memory than even the successes which have given him his little days of triumph.

The first big fish I ever caught is bracketed mentally with Mr. Spencer's song, for he got away in a pool just below the junction of the Mongaup with the Willowemoc, a pool where, as a boy, I often watched Mr. Spencer cast a wet-tail fly *upstream* with a long dangling dropper—harbinger of the coming dry fly—flicking the surface as it was worked across the current. There had been a small freshet; the stream was unwadable and the water still coming down heavy and discolored. I forced my way through a willow thicket and stood, somewhat precariously, above a deep eddy at the lower end of the pool. And my lure, it must be confessed, was a big yellow grasshopper which I proceeded to flip hopefully into the water. Something exploded in a flash of white spray against the yellow background. For the first time I saw a tight line cut an arrow on the surface, heard a reel sing, and felt an invisible mane rise between my shoulder blades. Then the line bellied, came back to me slack and empty, and I, too, went limp.

At the time I was but a beginning fisherman, and I may have and probably did exaggerate the heft of that fish. But experience teaches that it takes a good trout to make a reel sing, and, whatever he was, the experience stirred my imagination and stimulated an interest in the mysterious and unknown element in angling which has persisted through the years.

Here and there, there may be a fisherman who has "caught" and *captured* his biggest fish, but, even so, he cannot prove it. The heavy swirl that drowned his floating fly; the strike that failed to hold yet left him trembling as he retrieved his slack line; the shape which moved from shadow into sunlight and vanished in the fast water—any one of these may well have indicated something bigger and better than any of his heaviest prizes.

Despite popular and prevailing—if ignorant—opinion, anglers who come back with small catches but large tales are far from being the prevaricators the uninitiated would have them. Excitement and the opaque medium through which they view what they claim to see may cause some pardonable exaggeration, but your angler is of necessity a close observer, and experience makes him a fairly reliable guesser of fact from even doubtful and somewhat obscure indications.

There is a pool on the Beaverkill, known to carry heavy trout, where, due to cross currents, the floating of a dry fly without drag is a difficult operation. I worked up to this pool one July day when the water was crystal clear under the hard, revealing light of a brilliant sun and, standing thigh-deep in the current, began to cast to the comparatively slow water above. Nothing resulting, I moved forward and to one side, casting into the rush of white, broken water where the weight of the stream pours through a somewhat constricted channel. The fly alighted, bobbed for a moment, and drowned as the line tightened against something that came hurtling down in the fast current. Stripping quickly, I recovered the slack and bowed my rod against what seemed to be a fish of perhaps a pound weight.

And then it happened. Into the clear, blue-green waters of the pool, as if seen through the glass of an aquarium tank, moved a brown trout that I still believe to have been two feet in length. By some fortuitous combination of light and water conditions his vibrant bulk and coloration—even to red and black spots—were as vividly indicated as in some super-color movie of today. And this in a pool where I was fast to a fish which now, for a moment, I dared to hope was the weaving, gleaming crea-ture before me. But it was not to be. Into the picture, fighting the restraining leader, drifted a foot-long trout whose circumscribed activity was in marked contrast to the easy, fluent undulations of the big brown who hovered about with every indi-

cation of interest or curiosity—or, perhaps, hope of an easily secured meal.

————

The entire episode lasted but scant seconds. The big fish merged into a bubbly background and was gone; my trout was carelessly slithered up on a near-by gravel bank without benefit of landing net and somewhat scornfully creeled. But the picture I saw in Slide Pool remains as vivid, after a period of years, as it was on that July day and is mentally card-indexed as

one of several like and compelling reasons for revisiting, again and again, a stream badly overfished but still holding promise of conquests more likely to be dreamed of than won.

How much interest would an angler have in fishing a hatchery pond where the length or weight of the fish was without question within a certain, circumscribed limit? There would be little excitement, scant mystery as to what the water held, and no hope of the thrill of the unexpected. Put the same man on a small trout brook where the average run of fish is well below ten inches. Somewhere along that brook he will discover lurking places of sufficient depth and cover to harbor heavier fish, and he will spend an absorbing day in the attempt to prove that his intuition is correct. He may not prove anything by actual contact, for big trout in little brooks are cautious citizens and, except at night or in discolored water, are extremely critical of whatever in the way of food comes down to them. But somewhere, something is likely to happen to indicate the presence of a fish or two big for that brook.

———

I know such a brook; a beast of a trout brook to fish with the dry fly yet with a beauty and a charm all its own. From the spring at the top of the little mountain—where it begins its temper-devastating career—down to the river—where less adventurous souls pursue their calling with a calm and decent reserve—this brook offers five miles of the most varied long-distance, open-meadow and short-distance, catch-as-catch-can fishing it ever has been my good fortune to enjoy. In the brook, small trout five to seven inches in length are so plentiful as to be at times a nuisance. Along the infrequent open stretches a long and carefully placed fly will often take fish weighing three-quarters of a pound, and occasionally from the shelter of some moss-covered log or undercut boulder a dark-backed trout of a pound or more will strike fiercely and whirl back to his retreat. Seven low, wooden bridges supported on ancient stonework abutments cross this brook from source to mouth, and from beneath them enormous trout for a brook of this size—fish of from three to four pounds—have been taken, usually during high water and on bait. To raise one of these fish, or perhaps some other of like size in one of the deeper pools on the dry fly, is an event; to strike and lose one, a real experience; and to capture one, under the prevailing conditions and with four-ounce rod and 3X gut, would be the achievement of a lifetime of small-brook fishing.

Once, with a favoring wind and a tricky—if lucky—side cast I succeeded in placing a fly far beneath one of these bridges and close to the side stones of the support. Something lunged and drew back, and apparently, as the line tightened, I was fast to a terrier shaking a rat. Such pressure as I dared exert was of no avail. He simply would not budge and continued his savage and incessant tugging until the broken leader came down to me slack.

I never managed to raise this fish again nor did I ever hear of his being taken out. The following year, from under another bridge a mile upstream, a trout of close to four pounds was taken, during high water, by the proverbial farm boy in the proverbial fashion. This fish, when opened, disclosed a mole, two field mice, and various other delicacies washed down to him on the flood and may or may not have been the "dog" that condescended to entertain me for a few moments the year before.

There was another fish of which I spoke frequently and largely and whose later capture proved that, in this case at least, the truth was in me despite some more or less politely expressed doubts to the contrary. One of the best pools on the stream lies just above a meadow ford, and at the upper end the current comes down swiftly between the bank and a huge undercut boulder. Below the boulder the pool widens into an area of still, flat water on the right, while on the left the stream flows moderately and unshadowed through a gravel depression comparable to some giant's natural bathtub. Standing in the shallow water of the ford it is possible, by keeping the back cast high and clear of clutching willow branches, to drop a fly on the fast water and float it down without frightening the fish that lie basking in the current.

On this day, bright and sun-shot and with water low and clear, I approached the pool with unusual caution and was fortunate enough at the first cast to place a perfectly cocked fly where I figured it would do the most good. From the bottom of the bathtub a miniature submarine rose on level keel and, for a moment, hovered with its bow end directly beneath the down-drifting fly. Then, apparently dissatisfied with the observation, it flooded its tanks and sank slowly to its former station on the bed of the brook. I guessed that fish as between twenty and twenty-four inches in length, and the following spring he fell to a baby field mouse at the hands of another farm lad, was stuffed headfirst into a water-filled rubber boot and rushed to the tank in the spring house, where his length was discovered to be almost twenty-two inches.

I love that brook with its dark, over-hung ravine, its willow-guarded pools and holes, and its wind-swept meadows where a fly must be projected whole degrees from the line if it is to fall upon the chosen yard of water; where every cast is a complicated problem, where flies and leaders literally grow on trees, and where rods and tempers are strained to the breaking point.

It is possible, if legs and hands and nerves are perfectly coordinated and temper well under control, to spend a happy and profitable day along its banks and to return with a fair catch of fair fish as well as perhaps a couple of which you may be proud.

But it is the "fish that get away," those real busters, that draw a few of us back year after year and inspire us to dare the difficulties and disappointments of the brook in the brave hope of some day accomplishing the great conquest.

Once, in a pocket of one of the Beaverkill's swiftest rapids, I pricked a fish that wallowed like a broad-backed, black pig until the fly broke its too slight skin hold. On another occasion, my Fanwing Cahill floated past a boulder set in the midst of a perfect stretch of dry-fly water while a head, seemingly as broad as my palm, broke the surface with scarcely a ripple and as quietly withdrew.

Experiences such as these are met with yearly by anglers the world over. They are not confined to any particular brand of fisherman or any one species of fish. The sea, the lake, the pond, and the stream still offer almost unlimited possibilities—as well as the hope—for bigger fish than yet have been caught. And more and more, as civilization encroaches upon the wild places and as fish life decreases despite the efforts of state and private conservationist, the real angler is doing his bit by giving every fish a fair and fighting chance and by offering the big ones such odds as would be deemed ridiculous in any other sport. The linen-thread line of the saltwater angler, the increasing use of the fly and small "bug" for both small- and large-mouthed bass, and the adoption of the light rod and floating fly by the salmon man are outstanding instances of the newer sports-manship. But perhaps it is in stream fishing for trout with the dry fly or with a single wet-fly cast upstream that the worth-while quarry has the greatest chance of all.

The growing popularity of the three- to four-ounce rod; the use of the hairlike leader—a virtual necessity in clear and low water on our heavily fished streams; the increasing interest in the barbless hook and the tendency to present, at times deemed propitious, the tiniest of nymph- or midge-dressed flies—these are some of the self-imposed restrictions of the fisher-sports-man and his contribution to true sport and conservation.

If, occasionally, in fast and dangerous water or on some tumbling, brush-hung brook the angler strikes and plays and *nets* a really heavy trout, he has proved his nerve and skill and sureness of touch and may well regard his success as the result of patient and hard-won experience. But, whatever his fortune, it is safe to assert that he will continue joyfully to seek the unknown and the well-nigh unattainable. For so long as imagination tempts and hope persists there will remain that undiscovered star of the angler's firmament, that biggest fish of all—the one that gets away.

MARCH 1929

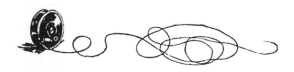

❧ FREDERICK WHITE ❧

EUGENE V. CONNETT III contributed greatly to America's sport and sporting literature. His Derrydale Press produced the finest sporting books and art ever published in this country; he himself was an avid sportsman and prolific writer. His knowledge of both woods and waters is evidenced by his work.

EARLY SPRING FLY-FISHING

BETTER TO COVER THE WHOLE STREAM WITH A FLY
THAN DREDGE IT WITH WORM-LADEN HOOKS

by EUGENE V. CONNETT III

THERE ARE still woefully large numbers of anglers who act on the belief that trout fishing in the early season is chiefly a matter of dredging the stream with worm-laden hooks. They catch fish, it is true, but they miss much excellent sport by eschewing both wet and dry flies in the heavy water which is prevalent in April.

It has been amply proven that this is an unnecessary deprivation, for in many brown-trout streams there is a well-defined period in late April during which the fish rise quite freely to floating flies. In the eastern Pennsylvania streams this is notably so, it being a fact that the dry fly is decidedly more productive in April than it is in May. I have no doubt that this applies to other streams of similar character in other sections, although it is not so generally true in the Catskill waters.

It is often amazing to see trout taking a small wet fly of unobtrusive coloration in heavy dirty water. One wonders how the fish can see such a thing as it sweeps down in a veritable flood. But they do see it, and, probably due to the fact that they have lain dormant through the winter and are now ravenously hungry, they take the fly freely. Knowing fly-fishermen catch more trout in April than do their brothers of the angle-worm. This is due, I am sure, to the fact that they cover so much more water with their hooks. The whole stream is available to the man casting a fly, while the bait-fisherman can only ply his worm in such water as the very nature of his cast restricts him to. In waters where there is a rise to floating flies, the angler could confine the greater part of his fishing to the very banks of the stream. Good fish will seek to place themselves out of the heavier currents so that they will be relieved of continuous and tiring struggles to hold their positions. They are not concerned with the depth of the water, and often lie in a few inches—just enough to cover their backs. These very fish are the fly-fisher's best chance, as they are near enough the surface to see floating flies clearly in the dirtiest of water. It is good practice, then, to cast the dry fly within inches of the shore, getting back under overhanging bushes, at times floating it amongst the grass on the overflowed banks, and paying particular attention to any spots where the combination of a quiet haven and a food-carrying surface current indicate the probable presence of a fish.

In streams with shelving, gravelly shores, offering few, if any, suitable feeding positions, one will do better to seek for protected spots around boulders in the open water. Because the water is roily and deep is no proof that trout cannot see floating flies. Experience shows that they can and do. Strangely enough, I have found that a bedraggled size 14 Quill Gordon wet will bring up fish, where a full-fashioned pattern of apparently greater visibility will not. I don't pretend to be able to explain this phenomenon, but I can produce ample testimony as to its truth.

The wet fly should, of course, be fished in the same place as the dry fly, but in addition it can be made to search out the depths by casting it up and across the current and permitting it to drift down free from tension, so that by the time it approaches the spot where a fish is supposed to lie, it will have sunk to a considerable degree. The sinking of a fly one or two inches deeper than it would naturally go if one kept in touch with it via the line and rod tip, will bring up a fish that will not notice it in the higher plane. It is probable, with the flooded waters full of matter in suspension, all drifting downstream with the current, that a fly moving across or upstream advertises its presence very efficiently. It therefore pays to work a wet fly as variously as possible around any spot where a trout is suspected.

Both in high and low water I have seen a sluggish riser waked up and hooked through the simple expedient of imparting a slight twitch to the floating fly as it goes over him. This action in no way resembles drag, but is a quick and sharply defined jump of the fly.

At all times of the year it is the small fish which most readily take either bait or fly. As bait is chiefly used during the opening weeks of the season because many fishermen believe it more effective than flies, numbers of undersized trout are injured and killed at this time. This, of course, is due to their having swallowed, either partially or entirely, the baited hook, which can only be removed by inflicting serious injury

Drawing by
Aiden L. Ripley

to the fish. Every angler who has the best interests of his sport at heart should learn to use flies in high water, and should spread this gospel amongst his less knowing friends, to the end that fewer and fewer little trout may be sacrificed needlessly.

————

I have seen men who turn to fly-fishing in May and June, kill in April literally every large trout lying on the bottom of a deep pool, by bottom fishing with worms. These fish are sluggish and thin at this time, and the stupid proceeding—which can't be dignified by the name of sport—of sitting on the bank waiting for the fish to pouch a gob of night walkers, is about the most short-sighted and pitiful performance I know of. These very men will cry the loudest a month or so later, when they find almost no big fish left in the streams to afford them good fly-fishing. It is to be devoutly hoped that this rotten practice can be stopped by law if not by education.

MARCH 1931

SAMUEL G. CAMP was an early contributor to our fly-fishing lore and literature; his books, The Fine Art of Fishing, Fishing Kits and Equipment, and Taking Trout with the Dry Fly, are in many angling libraries. Dry flies have lost some favor over the years, but—following the tactics Camp outlines here—a great sport can be had with them.

WET FLIES, DRY FLIES, AND REAL FLIES

by SAMUEL G. CAMP

THERE ARE three outstanding ways of tackling the problem of what fly to use. Ignoring entirely the natural insect life of the stream, you can show the trout certain well-known and generally successful patterns, and when these fail— as they sometimes do—you can fold up and go home. Or you may stay and "take it"—if you can.

The second method is to start in by offering a number of favorite all-purpose flies in rotation, and in case of failure—and only then—to give some slight attention to the insect life of the stream, with the object of discovering what natural fly the fish may be feeding on, and if possible showing them a nearly similar imitation. This mode of procedure has a good many followers, and it is a better way than the first because the fisherman always has "an ace in the hole," so to speak. It is faulty, however, in the following respect: Usually the game is

nearly over before the player suddenly realizes that it is time to fall back upon his reserves.

The third method is the safest. Also, I believe its followers get the most fun out of their fishing, not to mention, on many occasions, the most trout—or better say the *best* trout. Go to the stream without any preconceived notion as to what flies you are going to use, or whether you are to fish wet or dry. Let the natural insects of the stream take the place of first importance; observation of the active fly life will suggest what artificial it will pay to try—but keep the old and reliable Cahill, Coachman, and Brown Bivisible in reserve for use when all signs fail, as they often do. In other words, this third method is a reversal of the second.

At the height of the fly-fishing season, say from the middle of May to the first of July, insect life is apt to be abundant on the stream. In a good breeding season for the aquatic flies—depending to a large extent upon the force of the spring freshets, which, if of sufficient strength, may destroy large quantities of eggs and larvae—hatches of naturals are of almost daily occurrence. As the season moves on toward the hot summer months the insect life of the stream tapers off. This is a fact that the novice might note. There is probably a general belief among those who have not studied the matter that the insects of the trout stream are most numerous in the summer time, owing to the great abundance of insect life in general at that season. The

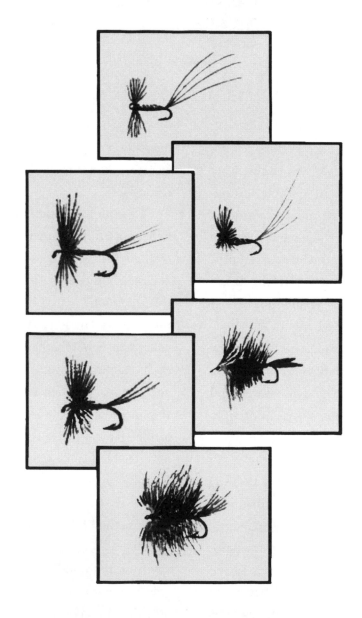

stream insects, however—those of chief importance to the angler—the May flies, stone flies, and caddis flies, are by no means so much in evidence as in the spring months.

If we arrive at the stream side, then, at any time before the coming of protracted hot weather, and after real spring weather has set in, we are pretty sure to see strong evidences of what is going on—or what *has been* taking place—in the insect life of the stream. That is, *if we look for these signs.* Some anglers, those who rely solely on certain fly patterns of proved attractiveness, are absolutely blind to the natural fly life of the stream. I know this to be a fact because as a novice I fished that way myself for a number of seasons. The natural flies meant nothing to me. As a result, I failed even to see them. I was too busy fishing!

If a hatch of naturals is taking place, specimens of the hatch will be seen coming out, taking wing from the surface or riding downstream with the current. This reference is to the insects of the May-fly family, and these are the natural flies that are by all odds the most important to the angler. The caddis and stone flies are of comparatively much rarer occurrence on the water, and as trout food they are of considerably greater importance in the larval forms than as winged insects. May flies—the largest of which is the familiar green drake—are easily recognized as they float on the surface with wings *erect* and held closely together,

resembling miniature sailing craft. These are the "duns" and "spinners" of angling literature. They are of many colors and grade down in size from the green drake, March brown, and other large varieties, to specimens scarcely larger than the tiny insects we know as midges. In their first winged form they are known to the fisherman as duns. Then, after a brief space of time, the duns undergo a further and final change to the spinner stage—the mature winged insects. These are facts with which, of course, the trained angler is already familiar, but perhaps they will assist the beginner in knowing what to look for—"stream observation" means very little unless it is definitely and rightly directed.

It is usually easy enough to capture a specimen of the hatch that is taking place, and then comes the matter of selecting an artificial fly which is *fairly* close to the natural in color and *very* close to it in size. From this it may be judged, and rightly so, that I am not a believer in the theory of "exact" imitation. It has been my experience, however, that an artificial fly which resembles in its general color scheme and size the natural fly on the water is very often a much better bet than a fly which lacks these approximations to the natural. Others may—and doubtless will—use their own judgment.

Select, then, if possible, a fly which resembles in its general color effect—pale olive, dark olive, brown, pale yellow, and so on—the natural fly you have observed on the water. The various quill-bodied flies—Olive Quill, Red Quill, Ginger Quill, and the others—will be found very useful. Quite often one of the popular all-purpose patterns—the flies we all use, such as the Dark and Light Cahill, Wickham's Fancy, Brown Bivisible, Light and Dark Hendrickson, Quill Gordon, and so on—will afford as close a representation as may be needed. In this last respect, however, the point is not to use these "popular" and generally very effective patterns blindly, but with some small regard, at least, to the naturals seen on the water—if, to repeat, you look for them.

As to size, numbers 12 to 14 will usually prove the most useful. These will come pretty close to the size of most hatches of naturals. Size 13 can be particularly recommended, but most tackle shops do not stock the odd sizes. It might help to note that flies on sneck-bend hooks are two sizes smaller, number for number, than those on Sproat, Model Perfect, and other straight-bend hooks—if a "straight bend" is possible. To play perfectly safe as regards matching the size of the natural, particularly when the visibility conditions are high,

select an artificial a size or two smaller, as, size for size, the artificial looks larger on the water owing to its opaqueness. But I advise using the largest fly that the traffic will stand—fewer strikes will be missed and fewer trout lost.

Lacking any visible signs of fly life on the water—that is, if no naturals are seen hatching out—it is still possible to gain a hint as to what fly may perhaps be successful by seeking evidence of what insects have recently been on the water—yesterday's hatch or possibly a hatch that ceased only a short time before your arrival on the stream. Drowned insects will very possibly be found in the little bays along the banks where small floating debris is collected and retained. Numbers of drowned flies are also usually to be found in foam patches, and branches that hang down into the water likewise collect derelict insects. It is safe to assume that the fish have been feeding on these flies, and that they will do so again if given the opportunity.

In the above we have had the dry fly principally in mind; this method is usually indicated when a hatch is on, unless it appears that it is really the emerging nymphs (larvae) that are being taken instead of the winged insects. The wings of the nymph

unfold when, having risen from the stream bottom, it throws off the larval skin while floating on the surface. Often—and especially at the start of a hatch—it is the nymphs, swimming up to the surface, that are most attractive to the trout. In this event—if your dry fly is refused and it thus appears that the fish are taking the nymphs exclusively—the remedy is obvious: Turn to the wet fly.

To capture a specimen of the nymphs is usually a difficult task, and particularly so in fast water. You don't see the nymph until you see the fly, as it might be said—and then it's too late. Generally the best you can do is to try any one of a number of nymph imitations known to be successful—or an ordinary wet fly known to possess nymphlike qualities, such, for example, as the Gold-Ribbed Hare's Ear, Mallard Quill, Greenwell's Glory, or Tup's Indispensable. Of course, if you are able to identify the nymph from the fly on the water, that is another matter—and one requiring more insight than most of us can ever hope to gain.

As a general proposition, when there is no active fly life on the water, it is pretty nearly a toss-up whether to fish wet or dry. I say this despite the fact that, under these circumstances, it is generally considered that the wet fly is strongly indicated. No doubt it is—but I have had some of my best days with the dry fly when I saw no naturals on the water from morning till night. I ascribe this entirely to the fact that the trout were there, they were willing to come up, but had nothing to come up for—except the Brown Bivisible or whatnot which I tried to show them with whatever skill I could summon. In other words, a straight case of no competition.

When there are no flies on the water and little or no evidence of previous hatches, if you prefer to fish dry, I believe there is no fly quite the equal of the Brown Bivisible Hackle. Mr. Hewitt, who originated this fly, believes the trout take it for a land insect blown or otherwise deposited on the water, a very reasonable explanation of its popularity with the trout on days when the aquatic insects are not in evidence. But whether or not this is the case, the Bivisible is certainly the *easiest* fly with which to "fish the water," the easiest to keep floating and to see, and these are factors of great importance when continuous casting on fast water is being done. A good size for the purpose is number 12—large enough to advertise itself well and not so large, as a rule, as to cause a wary fish to shy off. A number 12 Fanwing Royal Coachman might also be suggested. Other good patterns to use under the conditions indicated are the Light Cahill and the Quill Gordon, the latter of which I personally seldom use because it is so hard to see on the water.

A significant development of recent

years is to be found in the fact that some of our leading authorities are now on record to the effect that really expert wet-fly fishing requires a greater degree of angling ability than the dry-fly method, and that the pattern of the fly is of more importance in wet- than in dry-fly fishing. I use the term *significant* because not so many years ago, in what a noted angling author of a former generation sometimes referred to as "polite angling circles," wet-fly fishing was quite generally held to be somewhat on the same order as wife beating and allied pastimes. Wet-fly fishing is back on the map—and very much so.

That the pattern of the fly is of more importance in wet- than in dry-fly fishing is something which I have strongly suspected for some time, mostly because the position of the dry fly—on the surface—and its natural action are such as to impress the trout with its genuineness, regardless, within reasonable limits, of color or shape, providing the fish are not feeding selectively on a certain hatch of naturals. The matter of optics also enters into the question—a technical angle having to do with the

"trout's window," which need not be considered here—but it may be said that under certain conditions small variations in the underwater fly are more apparent to the fish than is the case with the surface fly, the wet fly being entirely within the trout's natural medium.

As already suggested, however, regarding the selection of the wet fly, it is very difficult to find out what is going on under the surface—often quite impossible in rough streams—and the best we can do is to experiment with the best-known wet-fly and nymph patterns. We can, though, go a long way toward ensuring success by using—when the conditions of visibility and other factors are at all exacting—small flies and leaders of the same length and terminal fineness as used in dry-fly fishing. Also, we can approximate the action of a drowned insect, or a nymph being carried downstream while rising to the surface, by fishing our wet fly *with the current,* allowing it to drift naturally downstream without—if we can effect this—any pull, or "drag," from the line.

MAY 1934

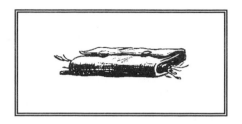

THE RIDDLE IN THE FLY BOOK

by EUGENE V. CONNETT III

ONE OF the reasons why I have been able to fight off the complete domination of the dry flies is because they are kept in beautiful boxes full of nice, little glass-covered compartments. At a glance one can see every pattern. Neat and efficient, but leaving much too little to the imagination. Snap up the lid, peek into the divisions, fail to see *the* fly for your present needs, and somehow you are bereft of confidence and hope.

Consider the fly book in which your wet flies are stowed. During the winter you have sorted out all your patterns and carefully placed them among the leaves of the book. By evening of the first fishing day the flies are well mixed again. Unless your passion for neatness completely eclipses your desire to catch trout—in which case you can hardly consider yourself an angler, particularly on the opening day of the

season—you stuffed a March Brown between the leaves which contained Coachmen, when you were hastily changing from the former to the latter. Some fortunate angler came along with several fish in his creel; you enviously inspected them, and respectfully inquired on what fly they were killed. In a somewhat superior tone you were in-formed that they were taken with a Gray Hackle. Not wishing to give the strange angler too much satisfaction, you waited until he had fished a minute or two and then, with hopefully trembling fingers, you opened the fly book to search out the magic hackle. So far as I can discover, no one has ever removed the old fly from the leader before taking the new one from the fly book. You therefore put the snell in your mouth, clenched the book under your right arm and the rod under your left, and then you removed the old fly from the leader.

Depending upon the character of your nervous system, you either dropped the Coachman into the stream while trying to get the Gray Hackle out of your mouth, or you managed somehow to stow it among the pages of your fly book—probably between the leaves reserved for Greenwell's Glories. Thus your orderly book became a fascinating jumble before the day was out.

Fly-fishing is somewhat of a state of mind: When you are confident, you catch fish; when you don't catch fish, you begin to lose confidence, and then you catch even fewer. If you have confidence in a fly, it does well by you. I am always confident that I have the right fly somewhere in my fly book, because I never know exactly what is in it. How different with the fly box: It is almost impossible not to remember just what patterns it contains. I have fished along for hours without a rise, but with the conviction in the back of my mind that the right fly would soon find its way to my leader. My state of mind was never for a minute upset by the thought that I had only one more pattern left to try before I must acknowledge defeat.

On winter evenings, among our books, how easily the subject of trout flies is solved. And how often. After reading Lord Grey, we know that the Red Quill will catch more trout than all the rest put together. Then we read Skues, and the matter is settled all over again, but to our utmost satisfaction.

We pick up Rhead, and to our delight find the whole question answered in a most comfortable fashion. Should we be fortunate enough to have a copy of Halford at hand, we imagine that the genus trout must tremble at the very thought of us. It is difficult to see why we should ever have had any doubts as to what fly to choose from our tattered old fly book. Just wait till next spring! We shall have to remember to be moderate and leave a few fish for other less knowing anglers. After an hour of delight with almost any angling author, we go to bed with mind at rest; we have at last discovered the right fly for our pet uncatchable. What a dismal shame that this dream fades when, on the stream, with rod in hand, we prove all angling authors liars.

I know only one contented angler. He has—at least, he says he has—solved the mystery of the trout fly. He uses a pattern that *he* can see when it is on the water: the Whirling Blue Dun. If the rest of us had as much persuasion in our cast as George La Branche, perhaps we could be contented, too. For myself, I should miss the speculative groping among the pages of my fly book; and I should detest having to feel that when the fish would not rise it was *my* fault, instead of the fault of the fly. Contemplate the painful necessity of knowing that the Whirling Blue Dun could do no wrong! Think how we should have to malign the trout—for it would be unreasonable to expect us to blame ourselves when the wretched creatures refused to rise to the paragon of duns.

As a matter of fact, not so many years ago I, too, settled the question of the best fly. I found that with a Cahill I could catch any fish that swam. But the thing began to be a burden; I felt guilty whenever the desire for a Cahill began to creep through my veins. Sometimes the longing for a well-dressed Pink Lady . . . well, I suppose the thing became like Tup's Indispensable to Mr. Tup: I simply had to give way and change flies. After a season of this unhappy state of affairs, I decided that there was more safety in numbers. My next circle of best flies embraced a full line of alibis, and if I couldn't catch fish it wasn't my fault. When the temptation to change patterns became so strong that it interfered with my fishing form, my conscience was quite clear—so long as I did not go beyond the limits of my list of best flies. The idea was that if these were infallible, it showed weakness on my part to fish with something else that was not so good. I looked back on the mental struggles I had endured for the sake of the Cahill, and I was encouraged to increase the circle of infallibles to twice its original size.

Nowadays, I have either insufficient mental stamina to wrestle with the question of best flies, or I am beginning to learn some of the rudiments of trout fishing; at

any rate, I trudge along on the theory that any fly which will catch a trout is the best fly—for that trout. This idea is responsible for much wear and tear on the old fly book.

I have often wondered, as I watched an angler choose the fly with which to start the day, just what processes of thought have led him to his choice. Is it the recollection of recent success with that particular pattern, or is it a composite picture of a series of angling victories extending over his years of stream experience? Does he fondly imagine that he is matching the insect on the water at the time, or does he consider the fly as being especially adapted to the present water? I have asked the question of an angling companion more than once, but have never received a lucid answer. The best I have been able to do is to search my own mind on various occasions for the most important points to consider, and the answer has been *the weather and the time of day*. Here is the sum of what much self-communing has brought to light:

If the day be bright, let the fly be dark;
If the sun be high, let the fly be small.
But here is a paradox you must mark:
The fly must be darker as shadows fall,
Until, when the stars are twinkling bright,
The fly must be black as the shades of night.
When very few insects are flitting about,

The fly may be wet and appeal to a trout;
But should Ephemeridae be on the wing,
It's dollars to doughnuts a dry fly's the thing.
Then when, prithee tell me, are light-
*   colored flies*
The proper creations to make the fish rise?
Ah, me! gentle reader, the answer to that
Is as broad as the brim on a Congressman's
*   hat:*
The most accurate picture of this I can
*   paint*
Is that sometimes they is and sometimes
*   they ain't!*
Unfavorable weather for dark flies, you
*   know,*
Is the thing that makes every last one of
*   us stow*
'Mongst the leaves of our fly books,
*   heterogeneouswise,*
A first-class collection of light-colored flies.

Now, if all anglers could only memorize the above lines, there would be less excuse in the future for angling authors to take their pens in hand.

Some years ago I was browsing among the sporting books in a second-hand bookshop, when the proprietor approached me with a small volume in his hand. He was anxious that I should buy it at what I considered an exorbitant figure. As an added inducement he fetched out an old, musty, leather fly

book, which had come to him with the purchase of a fine library. He offered to "throw in the fly book for nothing." He was an artistic salesman, and he won. The volume was a copy of Charles Bowlker's *Art of Angling,* published in 1814, and was particularly interesting because of the parchment leaves bound into that part of the book in which occurred the descriptions of flies. Actual flies had been mounted on these leaves opposite their description, but unfortunately the originals had been removed. The way in which Bowlker approached the subject of trout flies appeals to me as being delightful: "First I shall give you a catalogue, more out of curiosity than use, of those flies that are not worth the angler's notice, and so proceed to those that are more useful." Think of the trouble he saved his readers—and the money!

One day I looked through the old, worn fly book that had come to me with Bowlker. In it I found the story of its owner: The bright patterns—sadly mutilated by moths—told me that he had fished in the northern wilderness, and that he sought large fish was evident from the size of the brittle old leaders which lay coiled among the leaves of his book. He had visited salmon rivers in his day, said the Black Doses and Durham Rangers. That he loved the uninhabited reaches of the wilderness was proved by the bare hooks to which he undoubtedly resorted when his camp larder needed replenishing. I saw him as a middle-aged sportsman who had spent many years angling, for his selection of flies showed clearly that experience had taught him what he should need in the far-off woods. The fly book of a less experienced man would have contained a more varied range of patterns; he would have feared to go so far away from the tackle dealer with a restricted list of flies. Had our sportsman been one who angled on near-by waters, his small variety of flies might have led us to believe that he was a novice whose limited experience had inveigled him into thinking that he had mastered the riddle of the fly book.

And so we can read our angling companions from an examination of their fly books. We can trace their experiences on the stream by the selection of flies they carry. Stories of fine trout successfully creeled are to be read in the dozen Cahills; a lone Yellow Sally tells of disappointed hopes. Four Brown Hackles speak eloquently of the struggle which their owner is undergoing; he has been told about the virtues of this fly, but so far he has not had quite the required faith to prove it a killing one. Let us hope that it will be but a short time before we find a dozen in his book. A furtive split shot, scarred with tooth marks, rolls unblushingly out of a little pocket—how eloquently it tells of nervous moments in the presence of a trout too large to rise to a fly in the daytime! We wonder if it has any connection with the beautiful trophy, bearing a virtuous Coachman so realistically embedded in its lip, which hangs proudly on our friend's wall? Then we come to a pocket filled to brimming with a snarl of many patterns. If we have time to sort them out they will each tell its tale. The rusty-hooked, moth-eaten old relics are symbols of success; those with knotted snells, whose condition indicates but little use, are tokens of blasted hopes; and those which have never been wet are either emblems of weak moments at the tackle dealer's counter, or a remembrance of pleasant moments by the stream side in the company of chance-met anglers who swapped a fly or two, and made the day seem brighter with a trifling courtesy. An angler's physical stature might be divined from his rod; but if I were called upon to judge his mental qualities, I should try to solve the riddle in his fly book.

MAY 1927

JOHN ALDEN KNIGHT JR. was an angler and gunner probably best remembered for his *Ruffed Grouse and Woodcock* books, but his fly-fishing knowledge was second to none, and his Solunar theory revolutionized the sport of angling. His Solunar Tables are carried on by his daughter-in-law, Jackie Knight, and available from Solunar Sales, Box 207, Montoursville, Pennsylvania.

OCEAN TIDES AND FRESHWATER FISH

A THEORY WHICH MAY REVOLUTIONIZE

FRESHWATER ANGLING

"Having read the following article and discussed it in some detail with the author, I believe that further experience with and study of its subject may prove that Mr. Knight has discovered a phenomenon of unusual significance to anglers." (Eugene V. Connett III)

by JOHN ALDEN KNIGHT JR.

FISHING HAS always been surrounded by a certain amount of mystery. The age-old question—will the fish bite today?—has been answered with such a hodge podge of theory and conjecture that the angler finds himself lost in a maze of conflicting misinformation, founded for the most part on faulty observation and lack of real knowledge. To find a direct path through these winding trails of superstition and hearsay is a difficult problem. There have been many rules-of-thumb handed down from one generation to the next for the use of the casual fisherman— the man who pretty much takes his fishing as he finds it. To the serious angler these are not sufficient. The more actual knowledge he can accumulate, the better is he equipped to deal with the daily problems which confront him on lake or stream. To know merely that fish are apt to do one thing and not apt to do another is not enough; it is the "why" behind their habits which he must understand in order to obtain the best results from a day's sport.

Probably the most baffling of the habits of freshwater fish is their disconcerting practice of unaccountably "going on the feed" at odd hours during the day and then, quite as unaccountably, "going off the feed" again some time later. Every angler knows how trout, for instance, will begin to rise at a certain time in the middle of a June day in unanimous preference to other times, earlier or later, of equal apparent value. In illustration, let us assume normal June conditions are present—blue sky, bright sun, clear water, and a scattering of insects drifting on the surface of the stream with no particular type of fly predominating. For no reason that is evident to the observer, the trout may begin to rise at, say, ten-thirty. There is no extra or unusual supply of food present in or on the water and the identical conditions which prevailed at nine-thirty are present at ten-thirty and, to outward appearances at least, they remain the same until four-thirty or five in the afternoon. Yet the trout choose ten-thirty as the time at which they should feed on this particular day. As though at a given signal, they begin to rise in all parts of the stream, and, if one takes the trouble to check them, one will find that they all stop feeding with equal unanimity.

These feeding periods, which seem to be so arbitrarily timed, have come to be accepted both as inevitable and unpredictable by freshwater anglers, particularly the older and more experienced men. It is not an uncommon sight to see these old-timers sitting idly on the banks of their favorite streams, preferring to wait until the fish are ready to feed rather than to spend useless effort in casting over fish which are not inclined to rise. Experience has taught them that at some time during the day the fish will feed actively and that it is better to leave a good piece of water undisturbed until that time arrives rather than to alarm the fish by heedless wading and casting during the time when they are not on the move. If these feeding periods could be predicted with a reasonable amount of certainty for any given day, the angler would have a very definite advantage. He could then plan his fishing so that he would not miss the high spots of his day's sport and yet allow himself time for leisurely meals, the preparation of tackle, sorting of flies, and other necessary chores.

Fish are not particularly brainy. Their actions are guided more by the dictates of nature than by reasoning on the part of the individual fish. In attempting to account for these periods of active feeding which are so familiar to all of us, this uniformity of behavior indicated a common external stimulus. The big job was to identify that stimulus as, once that was done, then we could know as much about the probable times of their feeding periods as the fish themselves, with the added advantage of possibly being able to forecast these times from day to day.

About nine years ago, I had the pleasure of making my first trip to Lake Helenblazes, which is the source of the Saint Johns River in Florida. It was my good fortune to have as my guide that day Bob Wall, who runs a fishing camp near Melbourne. Bob had spent most of his life in and about the Saint Johns marshes and he knew those trackless wastes of water and reeds as he knew the back of his hand. That day Bob gave me an idea. He had so planned our trip that we should arrive at one of the few pieces of reasonably solid ground where we could land and eat our lunch at eleven o'clock. I questioned this choice of lunch hour as being a bit early, but Bob insisted, his reason being that the "moon was down" at about twelve o'clock. After some questioning while we ate our lunch, Bob explained his theory of the moon being "down" or "up" as the case may be. This was his way of saying that at some time during each day the moon crossed the meridian of longitude of Lake Helenblazes. If the moon was "up," he meant that it crossed our meridian overhead; if it was "down," it crossed our meridian on its return trip underneath. Bob kept his own "moon chart" on which he recorded the rising and setting times of the moon, and he had his own method of calculation to deter-

mine when the moon was "down." It was easier to figure when the moon was "up" as he could come pretty close by observation, but he kept track of moonrise and moonset just the same, so as to be able to check his observations and also to provide for cloudy days. Bob fished nearly every day of the year, and he told me that he had been using this moon idea for some time in planning trips for sportsmen by whom he was employed. He said it had been satisfactory, and it more than proved out that day as we brought in nine large-mouthed bass that evening which weighed seventy-eight pounds, most of them taken shortly after noon as Bob had predicted.

Bob's moon theory stayed in my mind, and I tried to apply it to northern fishing but it did not prove satisfactory in these latitudes. Not knowing why it applied so well in Florida and not at all in the North, I concluded that it was a local condition peculiar to that lake, which is quite near the ocean. The reason is clearer now, as I shall try to show.

The inability to anticipate the daily feeding periods in northern waters was for many years a handicap in a day's fishing, but it seemed that the reason could be found. Many anglers more experienced than I tried to answer this question, but they were groping in the dark and these talks were of little help. Information gathered here and there was carefully considered and compared with personal experience, but the same old question—why?—which lay behind all this refused to be answered, so I decided to disregard entirely what, for want of a better name, might be called the folklore of angling, and start from scratch.

In order to begin on a perfectly sound basis, only those things which were known to be true were considered, and a list was made of the known natural factors which affect the feeding habits of both fresh- and saltwater fish. The list went something like this: sun, moon, temperatures, barometric pressure, wind, seasons, available food, water conditions, tide, time, and so on. Each one of these items was carefully examined before being rejected as improbable. Finally, by the process of elimination, three items remained, which, while they did not exactly fit the requirements, still had enough possibilities to be examined further. These three were sun, moon, and tide. When applied to fresh water, the tide item seemed to be of little use, and that, too, was rejected, leaving sun and moon on the list. Individually these did not fit the necessary requirements, cutting the list down to zero.

Then the thought occurred to me that the combined pull of these last two factors caused the ocean tides. Could this same pull have any effect on freshwater fish? On looking at the question from this angle it seemed reasonable to assume that this pull is in reality the stimulus which prompts saltwater fish to "go on the feeds," rather than the actual rise and fall of the water level. If this were the case, why should not freshwater fish react in a similar way, as the pull of sun and moon would be felt by them just as plainly as though they were in salt water?

With this thought in mind, inquiry was made at the United States Geodetic Office, the Naval Hydrographic Department, the Bureau of Fisheries, all in Washington, and at the New York Aquarium. The first two referred me to the Bureau of Fisheries and disclaimed all knowledge of "inland tides." The Bureau of Fisheries was interested but could be of no help. From Dr. Townsend of the New York Aquarium came the first grain of helpful information. While never having heard of ocean tides having any effect on inland fish, he and his assistants had frequently noticed that clams which were on exhibition in the aquarium buried themselves in the sand in their glass boxes at the time of low tide in the ocean. At other times these clams would move about or rest on top of the sand. This was good news. Certainly, if clams, which are pretty far down on the scale of development, could feel the pull of the solar conditions which cause the tides, then freshwater fish must be able to do so.

Somewhat encouraged, I next called at the New York office of the United States Geodetic Survey where I had a talk with

Commander George D. Cowie. He was most helpful and not only answered my questions as well as he could but also furnished me with tide tables and told me how to move these tide times inland by calculating difference in longitudes in terms of sun time.

For two fishing seasons, a careful check was made of feeding periods against tide times. When other conditions such as adverse barometric trends, unfavorable temperatures, and so on were present, not much of anything happened at any time of day. On good fishing days, however, there was a marked indication of the feeding habits and tide times being coincidental. Being fearful of ridicule, I kept these observations secret, having made them more as a means of gratifying personal curiosity than with the idea of setting up a new

theory of angling. I noted, however, that my fishing had improved tremendously over former years.

After two years of trial in the field I felt sure enough of the idea to make it public. Accordingly, I wrote a story which was published in one of the outdoor magazines, having to do with a bass-fishing trip in Maine and incidentally mentioning observations of tidal effect on freshwater fish. The response was instantaneous and nationwide. Idaho, Wyoming, Utah, Texas, California, Indiana, Ohio—from nearly every state in the union came the request for information as to the method of determination of inland tide times.

The question of determining reasonably correct tide tables for various points about the United States is not an easy one. Tide times do not, as one might expect, move westward in the same ratio as sun time. There is another factor, known to hydrographers as the stationary wave theory, which has a decided effect as one goes farther West. Without too much detail, this is about the way it works out.

When the Geodetic office wishes to set up tide tables for a particular port on one of our coasts, the first step is to install in that port a tide-recording instrument, and readings of tidal fluctuations are taken for a year. Only in this way can tides be predicted, as each port has its own peculiar tidal fluctuations. This is known as the establishment of the port, and the port is then given an H.W.I. or high-water interval. This H.W.I. means the difference in time between the passing of that port's meridian of longitude by the moon and the arrival of high tide. There is a wide divergence between the high-water intervals of the ports on the Atlantic Coast and those on the Pacific Coast, that of Sandy Hook being seven hours and thirty-five minutes while Seattle is twelve hours and fourteen minutes. But by averaging these high-water intervals and then checking the averages against close observation of the feeding periods of fish here and there in the country, it is possible to determine with reasonable accuracy tide times for inland points throughout the United States.

So much for the manner in which the theory of tidal effect on freshwater fish was conceived. Let us now see just what this theory is. For purposes of clarity it is well to use a descriptive term or word instead of referring to "inland tides" or "the conditions which cause tides." For this purpose the word *solunar* has been coined. Solunar is a combination of solar and lunar and may be defined as follows:

The time at which the conditions which cause ocean tides (i.e. the pull of the sun and moon) pass the longitudinal meridian of any given point is the solunar period at that point.

Obviously, the actual tidal action in bodies of fresh water, with the exception of the Great Lakes, is not perceptible. To speak of tide in a trout stream is, of course, silly. By the use of the word *solunar period,* any confusion of this sort may be eliminated. Thus, the theory may be stated quite simply. It is this:

Other conditions not being unfavorable, freshwater fish tend to feed more readily during solunar periods than at other times.

This does not mean that the fish *will feed* during solunar periods. There are many factors which affect their feeding habits and their daily life. For instance, if there is a rapidly falling barometer or if the water temperature is too cold or too warm the fish probably will not feed, regardless of solunar periods.

These and innumerable other conditions make for poor fishing and nothing can be done about it. But when conditions are favorable and a good day's fishing might reasonably be expected, then the angler will find that the fish will come most readily to his fly during these solunar periods which last from an hour to two hours.

When an angler wishes to apply this theory to his fishing he must first determine the high and low periods of the true ocean tides nearest his particular section. Next he must determine the difference in longitude between the point at which he does his fishing and the point at which his tidal readings were taken. Having done this he may then adjust his tidal times according to the longitudinal difference between the two points in question by the formula: Fifteen degrees of longitude equals one hour sun time.

This method is satisfactory for the eastern states. Farther inland, however, the variation between the high-water intervals of the Atlantic and the Pacific Coasts must be taken into account. Admittedly, this is a loose method of determining solunar periods, but accuracy is not absolutely necessary if one remembers that these periods last for two hours. By approximation of corrected tidal times and some experimenting, there should be little difficulty in making satisfactory tables for any particular section.

Best results will be had while fishing during the solunar period corresponding to low tide. The fish will also tend to feed on the period corresponding to high tide, but this tendency is not so marked as it is during the low period. In addition, when it so happens that these solunar periods concur with such times as the early morning or the late evening feeding periods, then it is that the angler will usually experience the fishing which stands out in his memory as the best of the season. It is at these times when the fish take the fly readily and with hardly a miss and the supply of fish seems inexhaustible.

To return for a moment to Bob Wall's theory of the moon being "up" or "down." Lake Helenblazes is located on a meridian having an average H.W.I. of six hours and thirty minutes. In other words, when Bob fishes "when the moon is up" or "down," he is fishing on dead low tide. It is small wonder that Bob has the reputation for finding consistently good fishing for the sportsmen who employ him, as his extensive knowledge of the territory plus his observance of moon time render him almost infallible. By the same token, if the angler fishes on "moon up" or "moon down" in the Catskills, where the average H.W.I. is seven hours and fifty minutes, he misses the solunar periods by one hour and twenty minutes. It took a lot of time and hard work to find out just why Bob was right and I was wrong. Perhaps I should say that Bob was wrong and I was right. At all events, he gave me the idea, for which I am grateful.

It has long been my feeling that we know all too little concerning the reasons behind the behavior of freshwater fish. The more information we gather, the more forcibly is it brought home that the surface has barely been scratched. This solunar theory is offered purely as a theory for the reader to accept or reject as he sees best. But the fact remains that for the past four years I have confined my active fishing to these solunar periods, and the results have more than justified the effort expended in determining them.

The theory has now been checked satisfactorily on both bass and trout in Maine, Connecticut, Pennsylvania, and New York in the northeastern states. It has been used satisfactorily on large-mouthed bass for several years in Florida lakes and rivers. Last season it was checked again with satisfactory results, in Idaho, when the daily feeding periods of bass tallied with solunar periods with surprising regularity. Thus, in three widely separated sections of the country the theory has proved to be sound, and the probable daily feeding times of freshwater fish may now be anticipated with the same degree of accuracy as those of the saltwater fish, which is unquestionably a tremendous advantage to the fly-rod man.

JANUARY 1935

❦ JOHN ALDEN KNIGHT JR. ❧

PRESTON J. JENNINGS was an early angler who paid great attention to diet as it related to both populations and propagation of trout in streams and rivers. His extensive work *A Book of Trout Flies,* published by the Derrydale Press, has been reprinted and is a must-read for serious anglers.

TROUT AND AQUATIC INSECTS

HAVE WE BEEN PAYING TOO MUCH ATTENTION TO THE STOCKING OF A GREAT NUMBER OF FISH IN OUR STREAMS, AND TOO LITTLE ATTENTION TO SEEING THAT THERE IS ADEQUATE FOOD SUPPLY TO BRING THESE STOCKED FISH TO A CATCHABLE SIZE?

by PRESTON J. JENNINGS

WHEN THE British first settled at Jamestown, Virginia, in the year 1607, they found a virgin country and called it Virginia in honor of their virgin queen. The Native Americans, to whom the beloved Will Rogers used to refer with great delight as his ancestors who did not come over on the *Mayflower* but who met the boat, had done little to interfere with the natural development of the country. The forests which lined the slopes of the Appalachian Mountains were as yet untouched by the woodsman's ax; and the saw, the acid plant, and the pulp mill, which devices are the tools of the white man and of civilization, had not put in their appearance.

The streams and rivers flowing from these mountains ran clear and clean, and, being shaded by the forests which lined their banks, were cool. Floods which destroy fish and insect life alike were not known, for the reason that the forests retained the moisture and rainfall and gave it up gradually in the form of unfailing springs. These streams were abundantly supplied with fish life and with the aquatic insect life without which the trout cannot thrive.

The Eastern brook trout, or the speckled trout, scientifically known as *Salve-*

linus fontinalis, was the native fish of these streams, a lover of the shaded pools and cold water; even its name *fontinalis* signified that it was spring-born.

The sound of the first ax ringing through the forests was but the prelude to the great industrial development to follow, but nevertheless this first ax sounded the knell which marked the beginning of the end for the speckled trout. The ax and handsaw soon proved too slow to keep pace with the increasing tempo as the empire moved westward, and the water-driven sawmill was devised—an instrument of great power which was not satisfied in consuming the boles of the trees but also spewed out great streams of sawdust into running waters, killing every living thing in its course.

Sportsmen bemoaned the loss of their favorite sport of fishing, and sought means to replenish the supply of fish by artificial propagation such as had been practiced in Europe for many years, with the result that fish hatcheries were introduced into America.

No thinking angler will deny the fact that fish hatcheries have done a great deal to improve fishing conditions in our lakes and streams, and without them the average fisherman would not know what a trout looks like unless he happened to see one in a museum. While the fish hatchery has solved the question of producing fry and fingerlings, there still remain two important questions to be settled before we will have greatly improved fishing conditions. These are, first, intelligent stocking based upon water temperature in the main streams and not the temperature of the feeders, and, second, encouraging the natural growth of aquatic insects.

In an article appearing in the September 1935 issue of this magazine I discussed some phases of the question of water temperature and the effect the various temperatures had on the feeding activities of trout. No further mention will be made of this subject except to note that the question of lowering the temperature of the water in any stream is a long-range problem and one that will require generations to solve, as it entails the question of reforestation. In the meantime we should recognize the fact that a great change has come about in the character of our streams, and we should adjust our stocking operations to conform to present conditions.

In looking over a recent copy of the list of fish distributed in New York State for the year 1934, it is regrettable to note that the Eastern brook or speckled trout is still being stocked in enormous quantities in the feeder streams. In my opinion these feeders are not sufficiently supplied with insect life to provide enough food to bring the brook trout to a catchable size, and because of the high water temperature in the main streams the brook trout will not run down to large waters where more food is available. The result is that the feeders are filled with countless numbers of small brook trout, which have reached maturity without having reached a size which appeals to the average angler. It may be said that these fish are for the proverbial boy with the bent-pin hook, but it is hard to believe that the boy would get much of a kick out of battling with these four- or five-inch monsters.

Apparently the line of reasoning followed by those in charge of the stocking operations has been simply that water of a certain temperature is suitable for brook trout. Without taking into consideration the fact that more than water is necessary to bring fish to a catchable size, they have continued to dump into the feeders their annual allotment of fry and fingerlings.

I believe the headwaters and tributaries of a trout stream should feed the main stream with a constant supply of fish. This will not take place so long as brook trout are stocked in these feeders. There are many who regret the passing of that rugged individualist, the red man, but in spite of all our feelings in the matter, changing conditions move onward with an irresistible force, and if we are to keep pace we, too, must conform to the needs of the occasion, and the sooner we become reconciled to the fact that the brown and rainbow trout are the trout of civilization, the sooner we are going to get better fishing.

The second point which has been neglected, if not entirely overlooked, is the fact that the same agency which killed off all the fish in our streams also depleted the insect life. So far as I have been able to ascertain, no steps have been taken in the Empire State to rehabilitate the streams

{ TROUT AND AQUATIC INSECTS }

51

with the commoner and more prolific of these insects. To the average fisherman, or to the layman, the only problem seems to be the restocking of fish, but the fish culturist should and does know that water alone is not enough. Fish require an abundant food supply so that the energy they expend in collecting their food will not exceed the energy produced by the food they are able to gather; otherwise, instead of growing to a catchable size, they either do not grow at all, or, in the case of adult fish, actually shrink in size.

The Conservation Department of the State of New York has been conducting a biological survey for a number of years, the survey of the Champlain watershed having been completed in 1929, but, according to a recent communication from the Superintendent of Fish Culture, no attempt has as yet been made to transplant natural insects from those streams where insect life is abundant to those streams which for causes unknown are almost entirely devoid of insect life.

The East Branch of the Ausable River in the Adirondacks is one of the streams covered by the survey of the Champlain watershed, and this stream is representative of streams that have been stripped of their insect life.

The commonest flies which are to be found on almost any stream are conspicuous by their absence. Such flies as the shad fly, scientifically known as *Brachycentrus,* and the Hendrickson, *Ephemerella invaria,* both of which carry their eggs in the form of a mass or wad, could be transplanted with a minimum of fuss and trouble. From the general appearance of this stream, both of these flies should prosper there and afford a constant supply of food for the thousands of trout which are dumped in every year. At least, such an experiment would cost very little and might prove the solution to the problem of finding more fish of a catchable size.

The question of transplanting eggs and even nymphs of natural aquatic insects is by no means a new thought; this has been done in Great Britain for years, and with a great deal of success. Martin E. Mosely, in one of his books called *Insect Life,* describes the method of transplanting the eggs of the large May fly, *Ephemera vulgata,* which were collected by netting the fertile females as they approached the stream to deposit their eggs. The flies were held by the wings, and as the eggs appeared at the vent, the fly was dipped to the surface of a bowl of water, thereby washing off the eggs, which settled to the bottom of the bowl.

The bowl containing the eggs was then placed in the stream to be stocked, and as the nymphs hatched out they found their way into the silt of the stream bed and the fly became firmly established. He also describes an improved method of using submerged glass plates or panes on which to hatch the eggs. The exact procedure, according to Mr. Mosely, is as follows:

Since 1916 Mr. Peart has been experimenting further with the May fly, and has achieved so remarkable a success in the preliminary hatching of the eggs that it becomes desirable to give an account of his latest methods.

The eggs are collected by holding an impregnated female fly by the tips of the wings over plates of glass submerged in water. As the eggs appear at the oviducts the abdomen is brought into contact with the water and the eggs wash off and distribute themselves evenly over the glass plates, each of which is capable of receiving some 100,000 eggs, which is the capacity of about fifteen flies.

The plates are then placed back to back in a special wooden frame or crate, of which the sides facing the eggs are made of a fine-meshed wire gauze. All other apertures to the frames are sealed and no enemy can enter to destroy or injure the eggs. The crate is then moored in mid-water* to a stake by means of copper wires, and in the course of 18 to 23 days the eggs hatch and the young nymphs find their way out through the gauze into the river.

The shad fly and the Hendrickson carry their eggs in a mass, and it would not be necessary to go to the trouble of building special equipment to take care of the transfer of their eggs from one stream to another. The fertile eggs could be carried in a container of water and deposited in a screened location in the stream to be stocked. Eggs of the shad fly could be obtained from the Beaverkill in the Catskills, where this fly is abundant; and eggs of the Hendrickson could be obtained from the West Branch of the Ausable, where this fly appears in fair numbers.

Streams in Pennsylvania, which have few of the Ephemeridae emerging during the month of May, could be improved by the transplanting of the nymphs of the Stenonema group of May flies, which nymphs are easy to collect as they gather under the stones in the placid backwaters. On such streams as the Beaverkill and West Branch of the Ausable these flies are plentiful and

_____

*It might add to the safety of the nymphs as they leave the crate if it were moored an inch or so above the bed of the stream.

provide a scattering hatch of large flies during May and the early part of June.

For such streams as the Esopus in the Catskills the shad fly could be transplanted from the Beaverkill and East Branch of the Delaware, and the large green drake, *Ephemera guttulata,* which has never been seen on this stream, could be transplanted from the Schoharie, where it occurs in great numbers—and so on.

The Ephemeridae, as well as the Trichoptera, or caddis flies, are largely vegetarians and are suggested as being better for experiments in transplanting than the stone flies, which are inclined to be carnivorous, competing with the fish for food.

NOVEMBER 1935

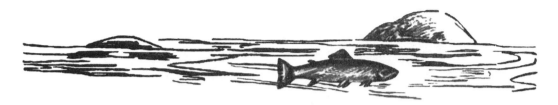

NEW TRICKS FOR OLD FISH

NYMPHS AND SPINNERS

by EUGENE V. CONNETT III

BROWN TROUT are universally acknowledged to be the most finicky feeders amongst the several varieties found in American waters. While it is possible to "gun up" an odd individual when no flies are hatching, ordinarily good catches are made only during a hatch. To the man who depends on dry flies alone, the presence of flies on the water, therefore, is an important factor. The wet-fly fisherman, however, enjoys additional periods of success, for he can often take trout when they are "down," and not rising to feed on the surface.

By far the most prevalent family of fly on which trout feed freely are the Ephemeridae, which embraces the May fly, March brown, olive, and other duns. They are easily recognized by their wings, which stand up straight and close together as they rest on the surface of the water. The great majority of our standard dry-fly patterns are based upon the imitation of this type of fly. Throughout the entire fishing season the Ephemeridae are hatching periodically. During hatches trout "go on the feed" and the dry-fly fisherman comes into his own.

Ignoring the period of several years during which the fly exists on the bottom in larval form, and lives chiefly on the underside of stones, out of reach as far as the trout is concerned, let us consider the period immediately preceding the time when it hatches out as a fly. It then comes out in the open and rises to the surface as a nymph, where it emerges from its skin, becomes what we call a fly, really a sub-imago, rests on the surface for a short time and takes wing. After a certain period it alights on some stone, leaf, or other dry spot, and slowly emerges from a skin, in which it has been completely covered. It is a fascinating sight to watch the skin slowly split and to see the perfect fly, or imago, gradually leave it. At first they are very weak, but in a comparatively short time they seem to gather strength and take wing in search of a mate. Having performed its breeding function while in the air, the female drops near to the surface of the stream and dipping to it in spasmodic flights, deposits her eggs. Both male and female then fall to the surface exhausted, with filmy wings outspread, and soon expire—having lived for several years in preparation for this final purpose of reproducing their kind during an imago existence of not more than twenty-four hours.

But, you ask, what has all this got to do with my catching brown trout? Plenty, Piscator. Instead of waiting until the subimago hatches on the surface, and the dry fly becomes the perfect imitation, why not take advantage of the fact that the trout are often feeding furiously beneath the surface on the nymph, as it rises from the bottom? Your wet-fly fisherman does this, and if his fly happens to look to the fish enough like the nymph, he "has luck," as the very inaccurate saying has it. Parenthetically, the more one knows of trout fishing, the less one believes in "luck," and the more sure one becomes of the fact that it is knowledge and skill that are responsible for heavy baskets of wild brown trout. Recently liberated hatchery fish must know all about luck, for they soon find themselves out of it.

The problem of imitating the natural insect with fur and feathers on a hook, varies greatly in the case of a wet and a dry fly. The former is either seen by the fish directly through the water, or as reflected on the undersurface of it—the undersurface being a mirror to the trout, except for a "window" directly over him through which he can see the world above the surface. On the other hand, the dry fly when not in this window, is seen by the trout as a group of flashing points of light on the under-surface, caused by the tips of its hackles pressing into the surface film, and it makes no difference whether it has wings or not— nor what color it may be. When the fly floats into the window, its form is indistinctly visible, and its color more or less defined according to the light conditions at the moment. It is therefore obvious from this very brief comparison, that the form of the submerged fly is more readily visible to the trout than that of the floating fly. It is the belief of students of the subject that the "luminosity" of the submerged fly is more important than its color, for just as a dog lives in a world of smells, a fish lives in a world of lights. (We will return to the matter of luminosity in a moment.) The logical conclusion must be that it is more necessary to give thought to the form of the imitation of a submerged fly than in the case of a floating fly.

There is one exception to this statement, and that concerns the flies which float with their bodies lying in the surface film instead of being supported above it by their hackles. Such flies are the "spent-wing" or spinner types, which are tied to imitate the imago when it sinks to the surface exhausted, with wings outspread.

We have seen that the Ephemeridae are available as food to the trout during three stages of their development: first, as nymphs rising to the surface, or being swept downstream by the current as they attempt to rise; second, as they emerge from their nymphal skins at the surface, and float on it for awhile in the subimago stage; and third, as they float on the surface depositing eggs, or exhausted with outspread wings as spinners, or in the imago stage. Why should the fly-fisherman confine his efforts chiefly to imitating the subimago period, when the trout feed just as heartily on the nymph and spinner? The answer is very logical: Usually he is not aware of the fact that the fish are taking nymph and spinner, even though he may see fish rising, for the nymph is beneath the surface, and the spinner is almost invisible upon the surface. Many readers will recall the times

they have floated dry fly after dry fly over a "rising" fish to no avail, when they could see no live fly on the water. The supposed "rises" were swirls made by the fish taking nymphs near the surface, or taking unseen spinners on it, and the trout at these times were not in the least interested in imitations of the floating subimago.

Rather than depend only on the typical dry fly, I enjoy fishing the nymph and spinner during the periods when the fish are taking them—or are supposed to be, for one cannot always know when the nymph is being taken. If a "hatch" is looked for about eleven o'clock in the morning why not fish a nymph until the flies begin to appear on the surface? At the end of a hatch why not continue fishing a spinner or spent-wing fly?

The nymph is best fished with as little drag as possible over or past the position in which the fish has been seen or is supposed to be. However, it should not be picked up until it has been taken down by the current to the end of the "swing" and lies directly downstream from the angler. At this point it should be slowly drawn in for a few feet before the back cast is made, for many a fish will see it pass by, and instead of taking it immediately, will follow it to the end of its swim, often lying just below it and watching it. When the nymph begins to move away from the trout, as the angler pulls it toward him preparatory to making

❦ EUGENE V. CONNETT III ❧

58

the back cast, the trout will often make a grab at it, lest it escape—presumably.

The spinner should be fished exactly like any other floating fly: dropped to the surface very lightly and permitted to float over or past the fish with no drag whatever. As the spent wings are often bent down so that they catch under the bend of the hook in casting, it pays to examine the fly at short intervals. In view of the fact that the trout can distinguish color in the body of a spinner lying in the surface film, it will probably pay to at least attempt to match the color of the body of the natural imago on which the trout is feeding, and definitely to match the size.

A word or two on the imitation of a nymph. It has been discovered that certain kinds of fur will produce the most luminous bodies for nymphs, and of these, seal's fur is the best. Many trout have been taken on nymphs tied with crewel wool, herl, or quill bodies, but from my experience with patterns in which I have used either pure seal's fur, or a liberal allowance of it in mixture with other soft furs, I believe it to be superior to the other materials. The tails should be quite short. There should be a very thin, soft, short hackle tied in at the head, and the body should swell in size at the shoulder or thorax. A fine silver or gold wire should be twisted over the body, both to protect the fur dubbing from the trout's teeth, and to break up the outline of the body into segments.

The day has definitely passed when the dry-fly man can look down upon his friend who fishes wet. Since G.E.M. Skues introduced the use of the nymph on the chalk streams of England, the "wets" have been coming back into polite society, as it were; and it becomes more evident each year that the truly skillful wet-fly or nymph-fisherman is a rarer bird than the skillful dry-fly man.

EDWARD R. HEWITT was an authority on both trout and salmon fishing. His books *Telling on the Trout* and *Secrets of the Salmon* are classics, and his later reminiscence, *A Trout and Salmon Fisherman for Seventy-five Years,* truly a joy to read.

A NEW WAY TO CATCH BIG TROUT

ALL ANGLERS WANT TO MAKE THE GIANTS RISE—IF THEY ARE IN A STREAM. THIS LEADING AUTHORITY HAS DEVELOPED A NOVEL TYPE OF DRY FLY, AND HERE HE GENEROUSLY TELLS OTHERS THE SECRETS AND METHODS OF HIS SUCCESS

by EDWARD R. HEWITT

In FISHING trout streams, particularly those with large pools in them, it is not uncommon to see a sizable fish leap from the water after a yellow or white butterfly; but it is indeed a rare chance when a very big one is ever taken in the daytime on a dry fly, such as is usually used by most anglers. After having seen this happen one day, I lay on the couch in the evening thinking it over, and it occurred to me that there was no reason at all why we could not produce effects with a dry fly, which would simulate the appearance of a butterfly, and get those big trout to rise. If this could be done, the sport of dry-fly fishing would acquire an added charm and interest.

Evidently, large flies of the usual winged patterns would not do the work, or they would be in use successfully for this purpose. There must be some trick in this which was worth investigating, so I experimented to see if I could devise anything which would accomplish the desired result. I had an excellent chance to try out anything, because in the Neversink pools near my camp there were a great number of brown trout running from two to six pounds, and I could always be sure that the fly was being fished over one, whereas in most streams, one could rarely know that there were any big fish to cast over and could be certain that they were never present in quantity. In three pools along my meadow I had, perhaps, fifty such fish, which had been raised and put there, and I was sure they had not gone, because they were seen every time the stream was fed.

The first attempts were made with the usual styles of flies, such as large fanwings and bivisibles of the dry-fly salmon type. These flies cast very badly on the light leaders it was necessary to use and often tangled the leaders up so that this kind of fishing was only an aggravation. A few trout were raised, but these flies never seemed to get the results I knew were possible with the number of big fish in the water. It soon became evident that an entirely new technique would have to be developed, if any large percentage of these trout were ever to be raised at any one time—unless, of course, they were on the feed, which every angler knows only happens for a few days each season. It had been observed very often that spiders fished with the bump cast, such as George M. La Branche has so well described, often raised large trout; but this only happened occasionally during the best fishing periods of the day, such as the evening rise or an early morning hatch. Big trout never seemed to come at the bad time of day, and I wanted to be able to catch them at any time, which, I reasoned, was quite possible, because they would take a butterfly at any time.

It was perfectly obvious that they would eat at any time, because when I feed the stream, which is done once or twice a week, trout always are seen to come for the food. They never miss a square meal, no matter what time it is offered. Is there any reason then, why they cannot be made to come to a fly at any time? Here was a real problem for the angler. Big trout will eat any time, they will take a butterfly any time, and they will take a dry fly only at rare intervals. It was not a question of pattern, color, or materials, as every known fly had been tried many times. No angler took more than occasional fish when they were feeding. The solution of this problem provided me with a most interesting summer's study, and I was almost sorry when it was solved.

It seemed that the fly which would be successful must be light like a butterfly and never get below the water surface at all, but must just touch the top and move rapidly over it. Thus, the trout would not have time to detect the fraud, if such fish were to be attracted. Years ago I had developed what is now known as the spider, which is a sparsely tied hackle fly on a very small hook, so as to get extreme lightness. Such flies, bumped over the water, had done better than anything tried so far. Then the idea occurred to me: Why not tie a spider fly on the same small number 16 perfect hook, just as large as the feathers would make it, and not put on any tail? It would thus rest flat on the water and not get wet because it would be so light. Such a fly, moving on the surface and slightly disturbing the fish's vision, might look to the trout, which could not see it well, like the butterflies they took so readily.

So I tied such a fly of a cream yellow color, using no tail. This color was selected because these hackles were the largest and stiffest of any available at the time. When it was ready, the question was: Would such a monstrosity cast at all? The fly was at least two inches in diameter, flat with no tail. It was rather sparsely tied, in order not to offer too much wind resistance. The only

answer to my question was to be found on the stream, so down I went just after lunch on a hot July day, the very worst time to fish. The fly was attached to a fourteen-foot leader ending in .006 gut, and an eight-foot, $3\,^7/_8$-ounce rod was used. Of course, the fly was oiled to keep it floating well.

The first attempts at casting this feather duster resulted in ridiculous failures; the fly simply refused to cast and would not drive or straighten out the leader. Fortunately, this same experience had been common when I was developing dry-fly fishing for salmon with large flies. They could not be cast near-by, but behaved perfectly

when enough line was used, so that there was sufficient stored energy in the line, as it was checked, to propel the fly forward. It was found that the large spider, which I afterward christened Neversink Skater, could be cast well if at least fifty feet of line were used—it went even better with sixty feet. With such casts the fly was easily put out straight. By using more force in the cast than was necessary for a straight cast and little more than was required to make the distance aimed at and raising the rod almost vertical, just as the fly was reaching the water, I discovered that it could be made to skip over the surface toward me. And by stripping in the line rapidly, it could be made to continue skating on the surface and never enter the water at all. The easiest way to fish was across the current, or even a little downstream. Upstream was found difficult, because it was hard to strip the line fast enough to prevent the fly from getting wet.

After I had worked out the method of casting in a somewhat bungling fashion at first and long before I had the proper technique, I could not resist having a try at a run which I knew contained six large trout. The very first cast gave the greatest fishing surprise of my life. The fly had fallen on the far side of the current where the water was perhaps thirty inches deep, with a few good-sized stones on the bottom. As the fly made two jumps over the surface, a trout of about four pounds leaped right over the fly, like a porpoise, and missed it entirely. Before he had time to recover, another fish, slightly smaller, repeated the maneuver. Neither fish touched the fly at all. Following salmon practice, I had sense enough to rest these fish and moved down about fifteen feet below them and tried again. This time another big fish jumped for the fly, and I just pricked him without hooking him. This showed that they were not playing, but would actually take the fly in their mouths. If the lure was handled properly, these fish should be hooked easily. After this experience I thought someone else ought to see the fun, so I dropped the rod, went back to the camp, roused my son from his book, and made him come down and witness the new kind of fly-fishing. By this time the first large fish would be rested and should come again. The fly was cast and drawn over the same place, but not pulled in quite the same way. The fish was given more time; I was learning rapidly. A big trout rose and this time took the fly solidly and was landed after the usual time. My son was sure he could do this stunt as well, or better, than I, and claimed a turn. He also jumped two fish and landed one of them. We kept on for an hour in this same run to find out if this method of strictly surface fishing would put fish down as readily as regular dry-fly fishing, or whether, as I suspected, a fly entirely on the surface, with very little leader or line in the water, would not alarm the fish at all. This proved to be the case. Only bungled casts scared the trout. We landed five of the six large fish in the run and hooked the other. The next day these same fish rose again, as if nothing had happened, and they seemed eager for these flies. This certainly would never have happened with any dry-fly fishing I had ever seen before—remember this was right in the afternoon of a clear, hot July day.

After fishing this run, we tried under the dams and found that big trout would come out and take the flies on top of the foam and bubbles, where it is most unusual to get any fish except with a weighted nymph cast into the falling water and allowed to drift down with the current.

In big, still pools this type of fishing is equally effective; but casting in such water is far more difficult, as it is harder to keep the fly on the surface. If the fly ever gets damp and goes under the water, it is ruined and must be dried out and put into shape before being cast again. These flies must be

in perfect condition to be serviceable, and few fishermen have the skill or the patience to keep their flies in prime shape. But unless this is done, fishing this way is no better for large trout than any other. So it is never likely to become popular or to come into wide use—it requires too much skill, too great attention to tackle, and too much time consumed in getting ready for a cast. Most men want a durable fly, which will give no trouble and which they can use for a long time on many fish. The Neversink Skater is a fly which must be absolutely right when cast, but is the best way to raise and hook a large trout where one is known to be.

When I am in practice I can often fish one of these flies for half an hour at a time without ever getting it in the least bit damp. Whenever a fish is caught, I always remove the fly and put on a fresh one and allow the old fly to dry thoroughly before using it again. So far, I have only taught a few friends to fish by this method; but I find that any skilled fisherman can learn it in a short time. Last spring a man from California was at my camp; the fishing with the regular dry fly was none too good, and no large trout had been seen. I wanted him to get some good fish and told him that I would show him how it was done when necessary. I had not tried the Skater method as early as May tenth before, but had an idea that it would work at that time.

I rigged up and raised six large fish in a few minutes, landing two. My friend became most enthusiastic to learn, so he could take this new idea to California. He was soon expert enough to take several large fish himself, and he has since had fine sport in the West.

This experiment continued throughout the whole season, and I now know that I can almost always get big trout if I have the right flies and fish well. Only when the water is clouded or high is this method of fishing a failure. Then a bucktail or a small wet fly is the right thing to use.

Here's another instance of its effectiveness. The president of the Anglers Club was at my camp for a few days, and we were fishing Yorks Pool with a dry fly. A few small trout were rising, perhaps ten inches long, but nothing worth taking. He seemed to think we could do nothing in this pool at that time. In order to save the reputation of my water I told him I would show him that there were good fish there, so I put on a Skater and waded out to reach a projecting point of rock behind which the large trout always stay. Two casts brought up one of the fish, and it was evident they would come. I got him to stand beside me so that he could watch the cast and the way the trout behaved, as he had never seen this kind of dry-fly work before. In a few casts I hooked a good fish and then rigged up his rod so that he could try it himself over more of the pool, as he had on long waders. As I remember it, he got eight fish, and I got four in a short time from a pool which had already been thoroughly fished with dry flies.

One will readily ask, why not use this fishing method all the time and discard ordinary dry flies? There are several answers to this. In the first place, the flies are not very durable and are a lot of trouble to keep in proper working order. In the next place, this kind of casting is very tiring on the arm and hard on the nerves. The constant attention required to keep the fly moving just right and at the proper rate becomes quite fatiguing after a short time. One longs to return to the old dry-fly fishing, where the fly cast easily floats downstream with no effort on the part of the fisherman. Besides, this fishing is not suitable for ordinary-sized trout, because the fly is too large for them to get in their mouths. It should only be used where one knows there is a big fish. I never fish the Skater except for large fish, and then only when I want to see them come or want to show someone that they can be caught.

The colors of the Skaters may be of any kind. At times a dark brown fly seems best and, again, a light fly or a Badger—it all depends on the light and water conditions. But one thing is certain; they must be large, and they must be very light with a small hook. I like them from one and a half to two inches in diameter if I can get them with good hackles. I have not succeeded in working these flies well with a short leader, but others may be able to do this where I have failed.

No previous description of this fishing method has been written, and I have shown it to only a few, as I wanted to have something of my own which I knew would work when all else failed, when other fishermen could not get the big fish. However, as my fishing days seem to be drawing to a close now and I rarely fish any but my own waters, there is no longer any reason why my brother anglers should not have the benefit of my discovery and get all the fun they can with it. But I caution them that they will not find such fishing easy to learn and to get results it must be done right.

AUGUST 1937

WILLIAM BAYARD STURGIS was an occasional contributor to *The Sportsman* in the publication's later years, and as this typical article reveals, he tended to let terms and techniques get in the way of fish and fishing. His words are nonetheless interesting for what they reveal about the equipment of those long-ago times.

HOOK TESTS
AND SILKWORM GUT

by WILLIAM BAYARD STURGIS

INVESTIGATIONS, AS applied to fishing, are usually the result either of sheer curiosity, of an outright need for more accurate knowledge, or of a healthy combination of both. Into the latter category will fall many of the findings of the future, for we already possess most of the essentials.

Take, for example, the subject of gut. We can all buy excellent drawn gut we know to be suitable for leaders. Yet, what dry-fly man is not interested in knowing the strength of each size, how it is prepared, drawn, and even stained? A fly-fisherman, to be a true disciple of old "Iz. Wa.," must have tucked away somewhere in him the propensities of a research scientist, a naturalist, and a philosopher. Is there ever a moment on the stream when he is not constantly pitting his wits against those of his artful speckled opponent in an effort to cir-

cumvent currents, obstructions, trees, and whatnot, to the end that the fly may float with such amazing perfection as to deceive eyes trained daily to differentiate between the true and the false?

What trout fisherman is not interested in knowing the strain each and every part of his equipment will stand, so that, at the supreme moment when he is fast in a four-pounder, he will have the assurance born of knowledge that the battle will be a fair one and the chances of victory at least equal? The more knowledge one has, the more skill one possesses, the more satisfying the pleasure when the day's fishing is done.

On a quiet winter's evening not long ago, in looking over Southard's *Trout Fly Fishing in America,* where he discusses the question, "How much can a trout pull?" (but which he proceeds to confuse with, "How much should a trout be *permitted* to pull?"), the idea came to test various sizes of fly hooks in an effort to find a precise answer to this question. Having found, by an exciting experience on the Wesseneau River in the Laurentians, that a 3½-pound Canadian brook trout, held firmly in the early rushes, can straighten a number 8 Sproat, and having seen a number 2 Model Perfect that had been sprung by a four-pound brown trout (both in relatively still water), the problem acquired personal interest.

The question then arose how best to conduct such a test in order to represent actual conditions. Some preliminary tests were made suspending a weight equipped with a wire loop on the bend of a hook, but this, alone, was obviously unsatisfactory. Next, it was decided that, other than using real trout, doubtless the nearest approach would be obtained by combining the results of two tests; one where the load was suspended from the barb, the other with the load hung from the bend.

In order to suspend the load from the barb, a short piece of one-inch leather belt was used, to the lower end of which was attached a bucket for receiving sand. The point of a hook was then embedded in the belt near the upper end, to the exact depth of the barb, and in such a manner that, when the load was applied, the hook hung in the position it would normally assume when hooking into a trout. The maximum

load capacity was determined when the point of the hook had sprung out to a position approximately 30 degrees above horizontal. It was found that, under these conditions, when the load was removed and the hook allowed to spring back, there was a permanent "set" in the hook of about 10 or 15 degrees. This approximated the amount of permanent "set" in the two hooks previously mentioned. The strength with the load hung from the bend was then determined in similar manner, except for the use of the wire loop in place of the belt.

By combining the results of these two tests (although the final results must remain purely empirical and assume the load is equally divided between the barb and the bend), fairly uniform results were obtained. Furthermore, it was thus possible to compare differing styles and sizes of hooks. Some may criticize these methods and can suggest a better way, but it is believed the results will be relatively similar and not materially different.

A fact, perhaps overlooked in the past, is that the weight of a fish *in water* is small, as evidenced by the knowledge that an exhausted fish sinks but slowly in the water when released. Its weight in water, compared to the pull it can exert when just hooked, is almost negligible. Therefore, the pull may be said to depend almost wholly upon the exertions of the fish to escape. When this is realized, it is incredible that the above-mentioned brook and brown trout, judging by the hook strengths shown in the accompanying table,* were able to exert a pull equal to more than twice their weight in air and, of course, many times their weight in water.

Another fact the table shows is the decided importance of using sharp hooks with small barbs, as the strength of the hook, when the barb is just entering, is only one-half that when the load is supported at the bend.

A still further use of the table is in conjunction with the testing of snelled wet-fly hooks, whether new or old. By suspending the snell from a brass upholstery hook and loading the fishhook at the bend with from one-half to two-thirds the amount shown in the table, it can be quickly found if the snell fastening is defective. Naturally, the

TESTS OF ALLCOCK'S FLY HOOKS—POUNDS DEAD LOAD

Model Perfect T.U.E.
No. 04991

Hook Size	Load at Barb	Load at Bend	Average*
14.	2.6	5.3	3.95
12.	3.0	6.0	4.5
10.	3.9	7.7	5.8
8.	4.2	8.3	6.25
6.	. . .	. . .	. . .

Model Perfect T.D.E.
No. 04991

Hook Size	Load at Barb	Load at Bend	Average*
14.	2.5	5.1	3.8
12.	3.5	7.0	5.25
10.	3.8	7.6	5.7
8.	4.1	8.3	6.2
6.	4.4	9.0	6.7

Slightly Reversed, Wide Gape T.U.E.
No. 6812

14.	2.8	4.9	3.85
12.	3.2	5.6	4.4
10.	5.6	9.1	7.85
8.	6.6	10.6	8.6
6.	8.0	13.0	10.5

Sproat T.D.E.
No. 1810

14.	2.9	4.4	3.65
12.	3.3	5.0	4.15
10.	4.7	7.4	6.05
8.	5.7	10.0	7.85
6.	6.7	11.7	9.2

Sproat T.D.E. 2X Long
No. 1810

14.	3.0	6.0	4.5
12.	3.5	6.8	5.15
10.	4.3	8.4	6.35
8.	5.3	9.2	7.25
6.	6.3	10.7	8.5

Sproat Ringed 2X Long
No. 777

14.	. . .	. . .	. . .
12.	3.2	6.3	4.75
10.	3.9	7.7	5.6
8.	4.7	8.7	6.7
6.	6.3	10.2	8.25

*The "Average" strength is believed to represent the approximate "fishing strength" of the hook.
T.U.E.—Turned-up eye.   T.D.E.—Turned-down eye   2X-long hooks are used for hair-wing flies.
2X-long ringed hooks are for bass and crappie hair-wing flies, when used with spinners.

*The writer wishes to acknowledge his indebtedness to Mr. Thomas Tully, of Chicago, for his friendly cooperation in connection with these tests of hooks.

snells, in each instance, should be soaked for not less than fifteen minutes before commencing such a test.

Gut for fishing, whether it be of the natural or the synthetic variety, is the deft product of the lowly silkworm. Although silk is produced in many countries, silkworm gut is manufactured in relatively few localities. The finest product now comes from the vicinity of Murcia, Spain, where silkworms are grown in large quantities for this express purpose. This work is done by the peasants, who carry on the cultivation in their own homes and, since the quality of silk and gut is dependent upon the health of the silkworm, the feeding, guarding, and watching of the crop is conducted with meticulous care.

The worm is, unfortunately, subject to varied and serious diseases, partly the result of propagation under artificial and simulated conditions for so many centuries. Among these ailments is one in particular called pébrine, which manifests itself by dark spots on the skin of the larva. Pasteur discovered this to be caused by a parasite, the effect of which weakens the worm. If the disease takes hold before maturity it results in inferior silk as well as poor gut. Pébrine appears to be not only hereditary but virulently contagious.

The silkworm, or larva, is a greenish gray or cream color and, when fully grown, is about three inches long and five-sixteenths of an inch in diameter. Its natural food is the tender leaf of the mulberry tree of which, during its relatively brief existence (of from six to eight weeks), it consumes an almost incredible amount.

Mention may be made here of an American silkworm, the large green caterpillar of the common brown moth (Cecropia). Knotless leaders, up to nine feet in length, have been obtained from these worms but, unfortunately, I have no information as to how the quality compares with the Spanish product.

Each silkworm is provided with two "silk" glands. These glands are long, tubular, thick-walled sacs extending along the sides of the body. In the normal course of events, when the worm reaches maturity, these sacs become filled with a crystal-clear, viscous, sticky fluid. If the worm is then permitted to spin its cocoon, the liquid is ejected from both glands simultaneously in one single, continuous thread through an orifice on the lower lip, known as the spinneret. The reelable thread thus produced is from eight hundred to twelve hundred yards in length and is one-twelve-hundredth of an inch in diameter. Oddly enough, the spinning is accomplished by the worm's moving its head around continuously for three days or more in a precise, sustained manner.

In the manufacture of gut, the fully developed larvae, when ready to spin their cocoons, are killed by pickling in either vinegar or acetic acid. This hardens the skin of the worm and partially solidifies the fluid in the silk sacs. Thereafter, the worm is split open and the two elongated sacs removed. These are gripped by the ends and carefully drawn out to their full extent, which may vary from 7 to 18½ inches in length.

A common practice is to stretch the strands thus produced between pegs at each end of a board, which is then placed in the sun until the strands dry and harden. The product is now known as raw gut and is tied in bundles of about one pound each and sold, by weight, to the gut manufacturers. At this stage, the outer surface is covered with a yellowish coating, or skin, which is removed by boiling in soapy water for twenty minutes. Following this, the gut is washed and then bleached by subjecting it to the action of sulphur fumes for twelve hours, after which it is again washed and hung in the sun to dry. This bleaching treatment greatly enhances the brilliancy of the gut.

The gut is now ready for sorting; first, roughly into three classes of thickness, then again into the various commercial sizes known as Hebra, Imperial, Marana 1st, and so on. When the sorting is completed, the strands are classified as to length and quality and tied into bundles of 104 strands each. At this point in the manufacture, there are five qualities, as follows:

1. Natural Selecta.
2. Selecta that requires polishing (called Mazantining).
3. Natural Superior.
4. Superior that requires polishing.
5. Estriada.

In order to have a neat appearance and to facilitate the polishing process, the hanks of gut are next stretched with the aid of two vises, one of which is slidably mounted and moved up and down by means of a screw. Those hanks requiring Mazantining are then dampened and polished with a dry linen cloth which removes the slight defects and improves the appearance.

The last step in the process consists of tying the bundles at both ends with red or blue string, according to the thickness of the strands, followed by assembling the bundles into units, or hanks, of 1,000 strands.

It requires from four to six weeks to convert the raw gut into the finished product.

APRIL 1936

HOWARD T. WALDEN II wrote this piece for *The Sportsman* the year before his second book, *Upstream and Down,* was published by Eugene Connett's Derrydale Press. This and his earlier Derrydale volume, *Big Stony,* were later published as *The Last Pool* in a number of editions worthy of your consideration.

STREAM LINES

"TROUT FISHING'S SOUL IS GONE," BUT MUCH AS THIS ANGLER REGRETS ITS PASSING, HE IS HOPEFUL, AS HE RECALLS TROUT WATERS HE HAS KNOWN

by HOWARD T. WALDEN II

SOME TROUT streams are important for their trout; almost all, for their beauty; and a few, for their associations and memories. In the last category are the secret streams of the past. Every angler, who has been at his sport a score of years or more, can remember the whispered directions, the pledges of secrecy, and the long, tortuous journeys to these segments of paradise hidden in the backcountry. Such prospecting and discovery once constituted the most glamorous aspect of trout fishing. But that is gone now, except in the remote semi-wild counties. Most young anglers, casting over their first pools in the 1930s, will not know the high adventure of finding a secret stream. The automobile has accomplished this special destruction along with its general spoilation of virgin countrysides. The motoring hordes have found all the streams there are. The streams are still there, most of them, but they are no longer secret. What was, twenty five years ago, the breathless private knowledge of a farm boy and two or three friends has become a matter of public information. The state has charted all the likely water, filled it with foreign trout, and invited the public to come and get 'em.

Of course, the public comes. Paths have been beaten by booted feet along both banks of the farm boy's secret brook, and the wild shy native beauties of that little watercourse are disappearing, dying in the hostile company of rainbows and browns. The age of science has been monkeying with nature. There has been, since the second decade of this century, much precise calculation upon the vital statistics of these grosser importations, *Salmo fario* and *irideus*. These foreigners have been welcomed to our brooks; there has been no immigration quota, and the result is the twilight of the native. Something essentially American is dying with these native trout, a quality that was rural quietness, peace, machineless enterprise, and nature left to herself.

Most of the truly secret streams were small, backcountry feeder brooks that were nameless and inaccessible, save by long tramping over the ridges and upland meadows, which lay deep beyond the infrequent roads. In such remote rills, known only to ourselves and our most intimate partners, the brook trout swam and lurked and met his chilly destinies, much as he had in the first days of the world. Some of these streams are still where they used to be, but not all. Man has proved that he can move a trout brook at will. In the name of progress, he has built his dams, made deep lakes of the little valleys, and erected his bungalows on the slopes where the deer used to come down to the stream to drink in the dusks of the past. Now on summer nights, the radios blare a foreign tongue up those long hillsides where the Little People had

known for ages the coon's cry and the booming of the barred owl. In the name of progress, man has straightened other streams into ditches, the better to irrigate his pasture lands or the easier to plow his buckwheat fields. And in the name of a still more illusory goddess, he has dried up his springs by deforestation and let his sweet water run forever out of his lands.

The devastation is not quite complete. Some of the little brooks have escaped it; a few, indeed, are as crystalline as ever and still whisper, in passing, to later generations of sweet fern, cowslip, and witch hazel and to the same live hardwood roots and, perhaps, to the same ancient windfalls we used for bridges when we were boys. But a change is upon even those. Their privacy has been violated. There are paths along their banks, footprints on their sandy shingles, and discarded trash in the bordering glades.

All right, then. That is over, the secret business, the magic of discovery, the solitude of unvisited waters—all that which was to me (and I think to most angling men) the loveliest things in trout fishing. It could not be defined; but it was what you thought of when you saw new trout tackle or when you breathed again the early ineffable air of another spring. It was trout fishing's soul—and it is gone.

Since it is gone, I seriously doubt whether trout fishing is worth pursuing any

more. That I keep on pursuing it is stubbornness, I suppose, or maybe a mere salute to the ghost of a sport that used to be. Perhaps, there will yet be a day when, around a bend of a remote stream whose beauty is beyond any words, I shall surprise something which will be that lost soul. Meanwhile, there is left to us survivors such water as has remained with us by the grace of a thousand circumstances.

Streams with reputations do not always live up to them, and the obscurer brooks often hold a big trout or two. The tributaries of a famous river are better fishing, at some seasons, than the river itself.

Fishermen, rather than the fish, perpetuate and enhance the reputation of a stream. By story and legend, by the magic euphony of a name, the prestige of a river is won and held. Beaverkill, Willowemoc, Neversink, Esopus, Lamoille—such names owe their celebrity as much to the tongues and pens of fishermen as to the numbers and weight of the trout between their banks. Those who have cast a line upon those historic rivers know them pretty well for what they are; the rest have their illusions. It is the old story of the prophet being not without honor, etc. An angler makes a three-hundred-mile pilgrimage to one of the illustrious watercourses; the day he arrives, a second angler—one of the local gentry who lives upon the celebrated banks—gets into his Ford and drives away from this great stream for a little fishing in an obscure tributary over the next ridge. The odds are ten to one whose creel will be the fuller at nightfall.

But I have no wish to disparage the great individuals among trout rivers. A reputation such as the Willowemoc's was not built upon thin air (though once the foundation was set there was no limit to the number of stories which could be erected thereon). Those who are the nobility of trout water have—or at least had—a high order of virtue. But it takes the intimate knowledge of long and close association to fish them with consistent success. They are big, long, deep, wide, and of many moods and tempers. Personally, I am a little uneasy in their presence, as if my meager talents were not sufficient to cope with their vast implications. Now and then, when the cubical air in my creel does not concern me overmuch, I can enjoy to the full the luxury of easy casting over the perfect stretches which such streams afford. In all the world, there can be no finer dry-fly water than a certain run well up toward the fork of the Neversink. A deep channel caresses the west bank for a full three hundred yards of slowly curving river. The east shore is a wide beach of stones, sloping with a gentle

angle into the water. In its normal stage in late May, the stream here is seventy-five to one hundred feet wide, and you can wade halfway across without going above your knees. The current maintains the mood of quiet: No white water breaks it, yet it is fast enough to give purpose and meaning to your dry fly's drift downstream and is so uniform in its speed that the drag need not be given a thought. Behind you is the open desert of stones; your back cast is forgotten along with your other troubles. Before you and across stream, is the smooth black progression of a noble river. You can work it from lower to upper end quite thoroughly in an hour. But there is no need to clock yourself. If it takes you all afternoon, you will be wasting no time.

It is well that such delectable pieces of water are not come upon around every bend of every stream. Like the high moments of life or of art, they should have the quality of rarity. They are the rewards of stream fishing, the compensating interludes of perfection between the long periods which are far from perfect. In one way or another, most trout water is stiff and challenging, much of it not less than dangerous. And there is no end to the problems imposed—problems of navigation, of casting, of the back cast, and the drag, singly and in combination. It is a little wearying in a long day upstream or down. To the man who has fought the current and been patient with hang-ups for hours on end, the emergence at last upon such a run of water as that Neversink stretch comes as a direct reward from the Red Gods. (Unless another angler—out for an hour's easy fishing—is there ahead of him.)

Yet, these mechanically perfect places may be of inferior productiveness. More than once I have overstayed the blissful repose of such water with never a rise, only to snag into a one-pound brown immediately upon resuming the battle with the rocks and rapids upstream. I have liked the theory that the easier the water to fish, the less likelihood of a strike. But there is no sense in my being dogmatic about anything in trout fishing, except the proposition that I cannot catch a trout under a bridge. A whole bridge, that is; broken-down bridges are different.

In that remote and gentle time, when life stood still in the clear air of the long afternoons, there was a collapsed structure—dating from some even deeper period of antiquity—across a brook deep in the woods near home. The road which led to it had long since been healed by nature, and the rattle of its occasional traffic had been buried deep under layers of time. It retained, still, a ghost of the form its architect had once drawn upon neat paper; its landward ends rested yet upon the dry earth, but its middle was intimate with the water. In the complications of its broken and sodden planks, a rectangular hole had been worn by the slow patience of the central current. A worm dropped delicately into that breach would immediately disappear in the unseen eddies beneath the remaining boards. There was, then, a moment full of such ecstasy as only boys who have fished the little haunts of the native trout can know and later recall—but never quite recapture. The smashed underbody of that structure was the favorite abode of the *Salvelinus fontinalis*. The sudden and violent strike would dip your rod fairly into the maze of timbers, and you would draw out from the wreckage a struggling and flashing eight-inch brookie.

Such places are beloved by the native trout. A fine fighting fish, a fish wilder and shyer, I believe, in its instincts than the rainbow or the brown, he prefers his water not clear and free, but cluttered with roots, windfalls, or the sunken wreckage of man's little enterprises. An old water-logged boat, a big tree fallen at last to the stream bed, the ruin of a bridge or dyke or dam—any obstruction which creates its own extraordinary eddies and backwaters—these are pre-eminently the places to look for *Salvelinus*.

Not that you will always find him there. Drawing a rainbow (or a blank) out of your favorite brook trout hole and hooking into a native in the clear sun-bitten rapids downstream are not at all out of character. In trout fishing, the instances which prove the rule seem scarcely more numerous than those which illustrate the exception.

One rule, however, which has a minimum of variation, is that big fish are found in big water or in small streams which are accessible from big water. The possibility of a large fish is present in a meadow brook three feet wide, if that brook has depth, undercut banks, an occasional deep hole, and no dams or high falls in its course to the larger stream it feeds. In one of my early ventures after trout, my companion hooked and landed a sixteen-inch brown in a rill so small that it could be stepped across almost anywhere in its half-mile course through an upland meadow. That brooklet, however, had all of the qualifications enumerated above. Other big fish have been taken out of it since, most of them as surprising to their captors, probably, as that brown trout was to us.

There is another kind of small stream, of wilder and more spectacular mien, in which you will never catch a large trout, unless the government has recently been by, heaving in the glittering contents of its cans. And that is not likely to happen . . . I mean those charging white and amber, rapids-and-pools-and-falls brooks which pitch down the sandstone and hemlock-bordered gorges of our eastern mountainsides. Even governmental optimism, which can stock the Bronx River with trout, stops

short of placing large fish in such water. Fishing here is a separate sport and a good sport, all enshrined in the mountain and the water beauty. You fish only the pools between rapids and occasionally a spot where the fast water jams into a back eddy or stills a moment in the downstream lee of a boulder. It is a lively game, a business of hazardous travel—where the hobnailed cruiser is better gear than the wader—and of welcome rests at each little pool in the steep descent. But you must be content with the little fellows, dark slender beauties of seven or eight inches.

It is conceivable that an industrious mink or black snake can depopulate one of these little pools of its trout in short order; but that anglers fish out this type of water is debatable. Such streams are hard to get at and hard to fish. The automobile will take a man within easy walking distance of most valley water but often not nearer than a mile to the upper and steeper reaches. In the valley stretches, where the few surviving trout grow big on much food, ample range, and plenty of protecting cover against natural enemies, man is most dangerous, and fished-out water most common.

That is why, of course, the rivers with big names disappoint many hopeful anglers every year. But the very reluctance of such waters to yield their big prizes constitutes a special challenge well worth accepting. And the water itself has still the eternal

appeal and mystery as it comes curving and crowding up to your waders, bearing its minute and variegated flotsam, its derelict insects, winged seeds, and suds. A million boots have plowed the sand and pebbles of this stream bed, a million flies have whipped its surface. It is old, old fishing landscape, scarred with its human contacts, familiar and friendly and kind to the childlike frailties of anglers. It will accept you and take you to its heart. But it will challenge your fishing skill today, as it never challenged anyone's a century back. Its fish are inured to the grosser solicitations of mankind; only the most deftly placed lure, the subtlest and most inobvious persuasion will win them. A Pale Evening Dun, dropped lightly as a thought fifty feet upstream, with wings cocked, without ripple from line or leader to herald its arrival, and with no subsequent drag to put its downstream course at odds with all the natural loose driftage on the breast of the current, will, perhaps, draw a rise, if a trout is there. A less delicate overture will put down any fish between you and a point several feet beyond the limits of your cast. But a hundred years ago in the same water there would have been no question about a trout being there.

If there is any moral in all this it is that we have some sort of compensation, hard to define, for the loss of the numerous trout and the virgin stream beauty of olden times. There is that challenge—which our great-grandfathers never were obliged to face—to a notch of fishing skill which they never had. If we have softened physically in three generations, our angling wits have hardened in that process. If we have less lovely places to fish in, we have far more lovely tools to fish with. The law of compensation has scarcely failed us, even in trout fishing.

APRIL 1937

THE CHAMPION WATER

TO THE FISHERMAN HIMSELF, THE LANDING OF HIS
FIRST ATLANTIC SALMON IS AN EPOCHAL EVENT.
BUT FEW FISHERMEN ARE ABLE, AS IS MR. KNIGHT IN
THIS ARTICLE, TO TRANSMIT TO THEIR READERS
SOME OF THE EXCITEMENT THEY FELT

by JOHN ALDEN KNIGHT JR.

MY FIRST salmon was the glorious peak of a pyramid of happy surprises. Just as a mountain climber makes his way from point to point, high ledge to higher ledge, finding the outlook more and more entrancing as he progresses, just so I journeyed through the years of reading and planning—through the various stages of realization of long-dreamed dreams—to the ultimate meeting with that twenty-one-pounder on the Matapedia.

Much of the charm of fishing is found not only in the actual happenings themselves but also in the pleasure of one's incidental impressions. For instance, my first impression of the Matapedia River was, and still is, that it reminded me of the Delaware. Some streams have a stern, unbending, forbidding, fish-me-at-your-peril look about them—dark water, heavy, dangerous rapids, shelving, slippery banks dropping off into deep water. Others flow through smiling valleys. Clear water, gentle current with enough movement to make for good fishing but not enough to keep the angler watchful and uneasy, wide pebbly beaches, rapids, riffles, and runs which are strong but not too dangerous to a canoe, all combine to make a friendly stream, one which murmurs, "Come and fish!"

Just as the Delaware is one of these latter, so is the Matapedia. Consequently I had a feeling of at-homeness from the first. Looking back, this very feeling of secure and companionable water furnished a perfect background for the whole picture.

My arrival at camp was timed for a Sunday, which is a rest day on the Matapedia. This gave me some little time to acquaint myself with the two-handed rod. At first the big salmon rod feels cumbersome, awkward, and unwieldy. Put it to work, however, and you will find that its proper use requires all the delicacy and a greater sense of timing and coordination than is needed for the light trout rod. My attitude toward this big rod changed, in the two weeks that I used it, from one of dislike to one almost of affection.

Monday morning dawned clear and warm, and with it came my first ride in a Gaspé canoe. These able craft are commodious affairs. In the larger rivers such as the Matapedia and the Restigouche, the canoes are manned by two guides. The bowman is in charge of the boat. The stern man handles the killick or lead anchor and does what he is told by the bowman, who decides all matters such as course, fishing, locations, and so on. The angler, not knowing the river or the salmon pools, has little to say about these things.

My host accompanied me the first day to instruct me in methods and procedure—

also to be on hand to "perform the ritual" when the first fish was hooked. "The ritual" is a custom of the camp. Where it originated, whose fiendish imagination first conceived it, I do not know. Suffice it to say that it consists of pouring a tin cup of cold Matapedia water inside the belt at the rear of one's trousers while one is intensely occupied in fighting the first salmon, resulting in a very decided conflict of emotions. But more of that later.

The water, too, chosen by my host to be fished, rejoiced in the name of "The Champion Water." Not the "Champion Pool," or "Champion's Pool"—the only name by which it was ever called was "The Champion Water." You who have never had the luck, nor the opportunity, to hook your first salmon, put yourself in my place and then turn your imagination loose to play with that name for awhile. *The Champion Water!* But then, aren't all the labels of salmon pools names to conjure with? Hell's Kitchen, Devil's Elbow, Cheater's Pool, Soldier's Pool, Million Dollar Pool, Mud Pots, Red Rock, the Looking Glass—names which by their very construction lend additional charm to an already charming sport. To hook my first salmon in "The Champion Water" was almost improving upon perfection.

A salmon "pool," so called, is a rather misleading term. In a trout stream a "pool" is a pool, just that. Such, however, is not

the case on salmon rivers. A broad defini-
tion of a "pool" in a salmon river is this: any
section, spot, or locality in that stream
where the fish are likely to, or do, stop to
rest on their annual trip upstream to spawn.
Consequently, a "pool" may be a pool (using
the term in the accepted or ordinary sense),
a long flat, a heavy run, or even a pocket or
series of pockets in a riffle or rapid.

The Champion Water is beautiful, to
say the least. An island is located directly
above it which divides the river into two
white-water rapids. A small trout stream
empties into it just below the island and
from the same side as the public road. The
far side is overshadowed by a rock wall, and
the river, after its hurried trip past the
island, settles down into a heavy, deep run

which extends downstream for a distance
of about a hundred yards before it slows up
over a gradually shallowing flat. The salmon rest here before making the trip up
through the rapids. There are always fish in
the pool.

We fished our first "drop" just under
the white water of the heavier rapid which
runs next to the rock wall. Before going further, let me explain that word *drop*. The
canoe is poled to the head of the pool, stern
first, where it is anchored by dropping a
lead weight known as a killick. The fisherman casts his fly at right angles to the current and allows it to drift until it swings
directly downstream. The fly is then picked
up and cast at right angles again on the
other side of the boat and again allowed

to swing dead astern. The line is then lengthened about three feet and the process repeated. For the first cast, a line of rod length only is used, and on repeated casts it is lengthened to the end of the casting range of the fisherman in question, or to the limit of the water he desires to fish. In this way, the fly completely covers a half circle of water with the canoe as a center or pivotal point. When the fisherman has cast as far as he can safely do so on each side of the boat, he reels in his line to rod length again and the canoe is allowed to drift downstream to a point near, but within the lowest part of the half circle already covered, and the process is repeated. The whole performance is known as fishing a drop.

Our first drop was fished out by my host, for demonstration purposes, but netted us nothing. On the next, which I fished, all went quietly until about my fifth cast. As the fly neared the downstream end of its swing, a dark shape detached itself from the bottom of the river and moved toward the surface. Having inspected the fly, he sank from sight again, leaving a hump in the water as though someone had pushed a kitchen table top upward under the surface. I felt a distinct chill and a prickling all along my spine and my heart kept trying to climb up into my throat. Before casting again, I decided to rest the fish and give him a little time to think it over.

I sat down and waited for about five minutes. Then I cast again. Nothing hapened. I cast repeatedly. Still nothing happened. We changed flies several times, used a finer leader, tried different methods and speeds of bringing the fly over him. All to no avail. That fish was not in the market, so finally we gave up and I reluctantly relinquished the rod to my host to fish the next drop.

All went quietly again for about nine or ten drops and we changed our location to the other side of the river. I had cast far out to the right of the boat and my number 6 Black Dose had settled nicely and started on its way downstream when I saw a slight flurry in the water and caught a glimpse of a huge squaretail for just an instant. Raising the rod tip, I waited for the line to tighten until I could feel his weight; then I applied the pressure and set the hook. The war was on.

Upstream he went—up and across the flat in a series of surging plunges which showed his dorsal fin and tail each time. There was no more chance of stopping him than there would be of stopping a launch with the same tackle. Nothing to do but hang on and apply as much pressure as was safe.

The casting line had long since disappeared and the backing was running low on the reel drum when he changed his mind about where he wanted to go and headed downstream. I regained considerable line

as he came down and passed me, only to start losing it again. Bill, the head guide, ordered "up anchor" and away we went downstream after him. Out of The Champion Water, past Indian Brook, through the Railroad Pool, he led us on an anxious journey until he finally stopped to rest in a pocket in the rapid just above the Ryan Water or Camp Pool—nearly a half mile from where we had first started.

The guides pulled the canoe over to the shore and I tried to pump him out of his resting place. He refused to move. I heaved and lifted and tugged. Nothing doing. My host climbed up the railroad bank to see if he could locate the fish from the higher position. Bill took one of the canoe poles and tried to scare him out while I pounded the butt of the rod with my knife. Still nothing doing. He just sat there and ignored me and my entire party.

My wrist watch told me that the fish had been hooked for thirty-five minutes. My host, ritual in mind, came down to the canoe and picked up the tin cup. He eyed me and the curved rod and the river with a calculating eye. Then Bill, the head guide, who had been wading about in the river with a canoe pole, saved my unprotected rear from the ritualistic bath.

He called, "Could you see him from up there, boss?"

There was where my host made his big mistake. He replied, "No, but I'll look again." So saying, he started to climb the bank once more, tin cup in hand.

It is my belief that Mr. Hewitt told me about this stunt; or maybe I read about it somewhere. Anyway, I had in my pocket some nickel-plated snap rings such as are used to hold a shower curtain to its supporting rod. Reaching into my pocket, I handed one of them to Bill and asked him to snap it around the line for me. With a dubious expression on his face he did so, and the ring slid down the line and disappeared in the water. My host had started to climb down the bank again with his tin cup and he was about halfway down when that ring slid into the surprised face of the sulking salmon. He had suffered indignity after indignity at our hands with admirable stoicism. Now, somewhat refreshed from his rest, he found himself faced with an added insult in the form of a bright little ring which pounded against his nose whenever he moved. It was the last straw. Upstream he went—through rapids, across flats, back toward The Champion Water. The two guides and I hurried to the canoe and poled rapidly upstream after the fleeing salmon, leaving my host stranded on the bank.

For the first time the fish began to show signs of tiring. This last run against the current and the drag of the reel had been too much for him.

Carefully, so he would not be frightened, I pulled him toward the shore. He was on the surface by that time, and hung on the line with very little movement. Slowly I swung him in where Bill waited with the big landing net. With a final flurry of spray he was on the bank in the landing net. The fight was over. Forty-five minutes from strike to net, and all chances gone for the performing of the ritual. Having killed my first fish, I stood immune from further threat of unpleasant attentions from my host and his tin cup.

As the salmon lay there on the bank, his silver side gleaming in the sun, the shiny shower ring by chance lay resting on his gill cover. Old Bill, the head guide, looked at the fish, looked at me, then shook his head and said,

"I see a lot of salmon come out of this river, but that's the first fish I ever see come to net wearing earrings."

JANUARY 1937

FISHED OUT

by EUGENE V. CONNETT III

I HAVE BEEN leafing through the pages of my fishing diary. On May 3, 1931, I wrote as follows: "I am seriously beginning to wonder whether the stock of large fish—over fourteen inches—has been terribly reduced by drought and over-stocking, as we have caught almost none of this size so far this spring. On the other hand, I have never seen so many nine-inch fish in the stream (the Brodhead)." When this was written I had taken sixty-eight brown trout, all under fourteen inches, since the opening of the season.

On June 6 of the same year—just a month later—I wrote the following: "I quickly worked up through the lower water and reached the foot of the pool where I saw a small rise in the middle in about twelve inches of water. I cast over the fish, thinking it was a very small one and had a feeble rise. I put a dry Blue Fox over the fish and hooked him. He made such a fierce, long run up the pool that I was forced to follow him, most of my line having been taken out. I supposed I had on a strong fifteen-inch fish. I continued to play the fish, which was unusually strong, and after about eight minutes succeeded in netting him. He was a brown, measuring exactly nineteen inches, the largest fish yet taken this year by a member of the club—or anyone else, as far as I know, on a fly. . . . Harry caught a fat fourteen-inch brown. . . . Never saw such a fine lot of fish as there were in the icebox that evening. There were more than a dozen fish running over fifteen inches. Edgar had caught a seventeen-and-a-half-inch brown. There are plenty of large trout left in the Brod-head, after all."

These two entries in my diary give some food for thought, when brown trout are concerned. Last season I visited a stream in Pike County, Pennsylvania, with a friend, and we saw just exactly one fish, a native of eleven inches, which was caught by my companion. A month later he again visited the same water with his brother, and they killed eight fish running from fifteen to seventeen inches—brown trout. On the first visit we had been told by a farmer living near the stream that all the fish which the state had stocked, before the season opened, had been caught, and the stream was fished out. But my friend had been there before when the big browns were running, and he and his brother went back later on to make the catch I speak of above.

Last spring I fished a club water in the Pocono Mountains all day, with several other men. I worked as I have seldom worked on a trout stream, until dark, and had five or six eight-inch fish to show for it. One of our friends went home in the middle of the afternoon, disgusted. I didn't blame him. I never saw fewer, smaller fish in a supposedly good stream. Less than a month later I returned with my son to the same water. He caught nine nice fish, and I quit after netting twenty—in about two hours. There were fish everywhere, and some good ones.

Well, what does all this prove? It

proves, among other things, that if a fair-sized stream has brown trout in it, and especially if it empties into a large river containing at least a few trout, such a stream is not to be pronounced fished out until an entire season has been spent on it. One week there may be no fish worth fishing for in it—as far as one can determine; and the next week it may show an amazing head of big 'uns. Big brown trout beyond question migrate up a suitable stream, and, usually coincident with the appearance of hatches of certain flies, will be found scattered along the stream in the best locations. I fished a stretch of the upper Lehigh in May and saw two little seven-inch trout during the entire day—and it was an open gravel-bottom stream where fish could have been seen as they were frightened out from the banks. In June, when the big green drake hatched, this same water was full of big brown trout. I don't know where they came from, but I think they ran up from the big Lehigh, which is a big river some miles below where I fished.

Anglers have been familiar for a long time with the annual spring run of big fish up the lower Beaverkill from the Delaware. I believe it will pay to study a number of other biggish streams that run into rivers not too polluted to hold trout. Years ago George La Branche enjoyed a fishing paradise on the "fished-out" Callicoon. He has

always told me to find a "fished-out" stream and stick to it. His advice is beginning to bear fruit, and I pass it along. June is the prime month in Pennsylvania for such experiments. Where there are rainbows in the watershed, business would probably open a few weeks earlier.

The first fish to appear might not be very keen on a floating fly—I'm speaking of big fish, mind you—and it would probably pay to start searching for them with a wet fly or a bucktail. When they are settled down in the stream, usually in anticipation of some good feeding on big May flies, then look for action toward evening with large dry flies. The local fly-fishermen on the Lehigh use dry flies that measure several inches across—and they take some monster trout on them.

I personally like to fish in June until it is really dark, not because of the finesse required, but because of the tremendous surprises I get every so often. Big fish suddenly appear at the tail of a pool where you have never seen a big one before. I imagine they have been down in some deep spot, safely tucked away from all artificial flies, and may come quite a distance to take up their positions where juicy big May flies float over them in satisfactory quantities. Well, I can assure you that when you hang one of these creatures, you will know something has happened—and you will remember it for a long time. You will also realize that your stream is not fished out of good fish just yet.

Our friend the bait-fisherman can and does raise the deuce with these big 'uns that are native to the stream, earlier in the season. I've seen him fill a hotel tray with them on the opening day, by still-fishing on bottom with night walkers in the largest pools. There's no law against it, but I wish he'd not haul out so many of them, so early in the season. This is one of the good reasons why well-protected club waters afford so much better fishing throughout the season; they aren't "scun out" by bottom fishing in April, when the big trout are on the bottom in a semi-lethargic state. When protected, trout wax fat on bottom food until the May flies bring them to the surface later on, and they are then in prime condition.

JULY 1936

ASHLEY COOPER HEWITT was a one-time-only contributor to *The Sportsman,* but his reverent words about salmon and salmon fishing are sound and—at the same time—lyrical. His advice is as valid today as it was seventy years ago, and his several books worthy of your attention.

SALMONITIS

---

by ASHLEY COOPER HEWITT

SALMON FISHING and woodcock shooting have a good deal in common. Both salmon and woodcock are migratory game; they are to be found in exciting quantities during one trip, and during the next they are—not. It is the factor of infinite variability that makes their pursuit so fascinating. No two days are ever alike, nor are any red-letter days ever repeated in exactly the same way.

I once had a day's salmon fishing when apparently every fish in the river was intent on suicide. It was literally impossible to make a cast without raising at least one. On a single cast I raised six different fish. So easy was their capture that I resorted to trying stunts. I had always had an ambition to catch a salmon on a Bucktail Mouse, and this day, after hooking four or five, I succeeded in landing one on this bait. Again, I

have known days when not even a rise was forthcoming. Sometimes it was because the salmon had passed or had not yet come in; sometimes it seemed as if they were glued to the bottom. On the lurid day described above a great many fish had banked up waiting for a rise in water before moving upstream, and I was lucky enough to be where they were.

Many things about salmon fishing— many "tricks of the trade"—I have picked up from experts; a few I have observed myself. I do not like to catch salmon from a boat, although there are, of course, places that can be fished in no other way. It is very difficult, and at times impossible, to place a boat in exactly the right position—and position is almost ninety per cent of the battle in raising a salmon. A few inches one way or the other make a big difference.

This is true of both wet and dry fishing, though it is more easily understood in considering the dry-fly method. When fishing wet it would seem that the fly must pass over the fish, and that that is all that is necessary. It probably does pass over him or by him—but how? Slowly or fast, in the light or in the shadow, going into the shadow or coming out of it? Hows and whys are as important as whens and wheres in salmon fishing.

Theoretically, the best travel for a wet fly is out of a shadow or from the obscurity of a ledge or rock into the brighter light, where it hangs almost motionless for a second or so directly over and a little ahead of the salmon, and then moves in a straight line roughly at right angles to the fish. It will be objected that there are few places where this cast may be made. The light factor is, of course, dependent on the time of day chosen to fish a certain pool or run, but the other details are covered by the method of making the cast. This is why position is so important. The usual method is to cast across the current at from 60 to 45 degrees and allow the fly to swing as it will in the current; but I prefer to make this cast quite differently.

Let us take a hypothetical case. I am going to fish the head of a pool which has a run along a ledge of rocks. The run may be anywhere from two to eight or more feet deep. The sun is on the right side as one faces downstream, throwing a shadow several feet out from the ledge. I start in well above where there should be any salmon—because often they are where they should not be, and in quite shallow water. The cast is made directly across the current or, if anything, a little upstream—not straight, but so that the fly drops upstream of the line and very close to the ledge—within two inches of it. The pull of the line makes the fly travel very rapidly along the ledge for a couple of feet and then swing out with a snap-the-whip action, causing it to hang almost stationary for a second or so. It will then start to swing in an arc toward me. I make it follow a straight line instead of an arc by stripping in the line with the left hand. The run is fished down in this manner, my position in respect to the current varying so as to bring the point of the hang or "dwell" at the proper place. Quite slow-moving currents can be fished this way, by the careful use of the left hand in stripping in the line. I have never been able to make this cast well with the two-handed rod, but that is probably because I have used a single-handed rod more and like it better.

Another important feature in fishing with a wet fly according to this method is to keep the fly traveling after the dwell at a constant speed. This is accomplished by stripping in the line and raising the rod. I have tested the rate of speed of the fly many times and have always found

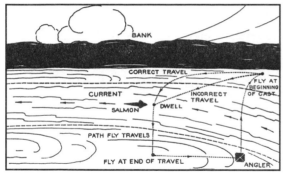

The conventional wet-fly cast

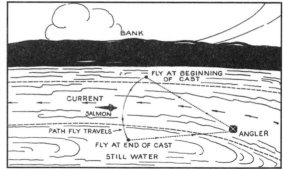

The author's wet-fly cast

that a uniformly slow rate brings the best results. This may be tried out by changing the speed when a salmon is seen following the fly; in the majority of cases he will turn away from it.

The smaller rivers that can be waded are best suited to this type of fishing, although I have used it in large waters, casting from a boat. It is almost essential to use light tackle and a single-handed rod, as this can be manipulated so much more easily and delicately. There is seldom any trouble handling a fish on this tackle if there is enough fine backing to the line. I like about 200 yards back of the casting line; before he has run this out I can usually get out on the bank and follow him, or, if necessary, use the boat. A fish is tired out, not by the pull on him, but by his own violent exertions. The more he can be kept moving, the sooner he can be landed. Occasionally, a sulky fish that just hangs in one place on the bottom will be hooked. He can often be stirred up by changing

the direction of the pull, as fish will usually go the opposite way from the pull. Sometimes, however, you will have to throw rocks at him or have the guide poke him with the pole. The main thing is to get action, and plenty of it, if you want to tire the fish quickly.

As to the flies themselves: They seem to vary in different rivers. I do not think that the pattern itself has as much to do with their effectiveness as have the size and shape and general color scheme. In our river the salmon apparently like long, slinky, skinny flies, while in Newfoundland on the east coast they prefer smaller, chunkier flies. I have caught salmon in the Restigouche on ordinary trout wet flies as small as size 14. In our river I have used flies up to three inches long. In order to cast these larger flies on light tackle, special light, long-shanked hooks had to be used. As I tie most of my own flies on the river, they have no names or definite patterns. The one feather which seems to help in any fly is the well-known jungle cock ruff. Instead of the usual feather hackle, I use silver tinsel thread; gold tinsel does not seem to be much good. Almost all of the standard patterns are useful, but in the large sizes they cannot be well handled on a light rod and leader.

The *crème de la crème* of salmon fishing is, of course, dry-fly fishing. This requires a high degree of skill and knowledge and a very perfect and specialized equipment. It requires great accuracy in laying the fly where you want it and as you want it—or, rather, as the fish want it. In this fishing perfect balance of the tackle is essential— the line to the rod, the leader to the line, the reel to the rod, and so on. It is almost impossible to describe this balance in writing, as each rig is different. When it is right, the fly seems to go out with no effort on your part. The best test I know is to see how much line can be shot through the guides from coils held loosely in the left hand. With a well-balanced rig, twenty to thirty feet of line can be shot through the guides. The best flies are the hackles, preferably Tied Palmer. Winged flies in these larger sizes are likely to whirl and ball up the leader. There is nothing quite like the thrill of seeing your fish and then fishing for him, cast after cast, until he comes up for the fly. Sometimes he will come with a rush; at other times, he sidles up to it; again, he will even jump for it.

Salmon are often caught in queer places. I have caught them in still, pondlike holes covered with lily pads. Beware light tackle here when they start cutting up! I have taken them out of little, deep potholes. I once took a twenty-six-pound fish out of a gravel stretch where there was a hole in under a grass bank not more than ten feet long and eight feet wide. He came out for the fly just like a brook trout. In one of his rushes he ran himself up on the beach, or I should never have got him. I have caught them in the outlet of a lake on a piece of trout belly while fishing for sea trout. Fresh-run salmon will often take this bait. It is hard to catch salmon just below falls; they seem to have their minds intent on getting over the falls.

One story of the usual big fish that got away will illustrate the excitement of the game. On my last trip to the Matapedia I hooked into a big fish one evening. I was using light tackle and had to fish the pool from a boat. He came toward me and shook out the fly. I decided to give him a try the following morning. I used my big two-handed rod and a heavy leader, as I wanted to fish on my feet and be ready to run, and I could not quite reach him with the single-handed rod. He took it with a rush and I hooked him well. After a short run he sulked—for which I was glad, as it gave me time to get to shore. I could not move him by pulling or throwing rocks. I climbed into the canoe and the guide shoved out to stir him up with the pole. He moved, all right. He cut a figure eight around the canoe so fast that he had me in contortions to keep from breaking the rod. Then he went upstream like a shot, and I could feel he had gone under something. Just as the line came to the backing splice it broke. Nothing to do but swear. While I was rigging up again I asked the guide to see if he could discern the line. He soon spied it, fished up the end of it with the pole, and brought it in. I pulled on it and felt the fish still on it, sulking again. What to do? I could not tie a knot, as it would not run through the guides in a rush. I got out the rod repair kit and made a splice with waxed thread—not an easy thing to do in my state of excitement and with hands not too steady. I made a splice of sorts that I hoped would hold, and reeled in. He was still on. I made ready for action, and told the guide to have the canoe at hand in case the fish went down out of the pool. I raised the rod to put the strain on him. He was still on. I put on the strain, and he acted as if he were going to make a rush. He came to the top of the water and made one turn—and the fly pulled out.

Salmonitis, once contracted, is incurable. There is no other sport which seems to have so irresistible a lure as fishing, and

there is no fishing that can quite touch salmon fishing. As Sir Edward Grey says of it in *Fly Fishing,* we may not all feel for it that intimate affection which we do for some other forms of angling, but the greatness of it as a sport is indisputable, and we admit its supremacy. "There is an exhilaration and excitement and mystery about it," he writes, "the thought of which hurries us toward any opportunity of angling on a river which is known to hold salmon. . . . The supreme moment is undoubtedly the actual hooking of the fish. However great one's expectation and keenness, the feel of the fish when it hooks itself comes always with a shock of surprise and delight, and there is a sudden thrill in having to do with the weight and strength of a salmon. A sense of complete achievement and satisfaction is felt merely in the hooking of it, and it is a satisfaction that remains undiminished as years go on. In all sport, there is nothing to equal the glory of success in salmon fishing."

Salmon has been fished with rod and reel in England for at least two centuries. Izaak Walton speaks of it as the "king of fresh water fishes" and in referring to salmon tackle says: "Note also that many used to fish for salmon with a ring of wire on the top of their rod; through which the line may run to as great a length as is needful, when it is hooked. And to that end some use a wheel about the middle of their rod, or near their hand." This was in 1670 or thereabouts. The number of books written since then partly or wholly on salmon would fill a library, for, of course, the fish itself is a fascinating study, aside from its interest to the angler. And the quality of its interest to the angler only an angler can understand.

JUNE 1927

HENRY MARION HALL, an outdoor writer conversant with the fields and streams of the past, wrote several books. His expertise is perhaps slanted toward grouse and woodcock, but this short article is pointed and poignant, and a welcome pause between the preachings of others.

THOSE FUGITIVE TROUT

THE ONES THAT GET AWAY ARE NEVER LOST;
THEY GROW LARGER AS THE
MEMORY OF THEM IS RECALLED

---

by HENRY MARION HALL

No matter how many trout an angler may land, those big fellows which break away sometimes make the most lasting impression. They do not shrink, like their captured brethren in the creel, but grow miraculously larger and brighter in memory. Their loss is never complete. Even after years, they have a trick of rising from the embers of a camp fire to snap at phantom flies.

Such was that royal rainbow, by far the best in a decade, which I once hooked, played, and tired in midstream. One moment he turned his broad and jeweled flank to the sun; the next he was in the net; and the last he staged a spasm just when I was unhooking him. Even today, I cannot forgive myself for letting that prize writhe out of my grip to swirl into the deeps. It proved somewhat the same with a famous brown trout in an overfished pool below a stone mill on the Raritan. Several of us struck him last spring, but only to feel the monster bolt like a muskellunge and snap the leader. Then one Sabbath, when he should have been in church, a boy with a heavy steel rod casually derricked him and gloried in the feat.

Camp-fire chat would languish without last-minute losses. Everybody bemoans some particular fish, lost through a lapse in technique, but certainly worthy of glittering in the constellation Pisces. Formerly, such delusions mildly amused me, but since a certain trip, I too, must tell my tale.

A friend and I were fishing a brook

99

which twists through burned slash in northern Ontario, a nightmare of charred logs, fire-hardened spikes, and windfalls where even the stream could barely squeeze a way. Squaretails haunted every hole and led us into formidable trouble. Once in the heart of that jungle, however, we refused to retreat, but persisted until we emerged into a green world of fir.

After our struggles in the sooty wilderness, it seemed a bit of paradise. Evergreens breathed sweet, the hermit thrush chanted, and spruce grouse whirred up while we jointed our rods. The spoor of a moose led us to stilly basins, moss-rimmed and gay with northern lilies. The deep water was alive with fish, apparently ignorant of the wiles of man, or else extremely hungry. At any rate, they were much tamer than fish in more southern waters. Curiously enough, however, they rejected the Parmacheene Belle, Red Ibis, and other brilliant lures, so effective elsewhere in the province, but took a fancy to a faded Jenny Lind, one of two in my book, but a fly seldom used by either of us. Eleven noble char succumbed to this whimsey, among them one really superb swimmer.

Nevertheless, my recollection of that rivulet is somber. On the tramp back to camp my eye fell on a pothole simmering between fallen trunks in a thicket—a place swarming with trout, but so well protected by obstacles as to render it difficult to take any. Allowing the Jenny to drift under impending branches, I contrived to strike several lively fish, but promptly lost them. It was tantalizing work, and I would not have kept on, but for an extraordinary apparition.

I was turning to quit the brook, when suddenly a mottled back loomed in the trembling deeps—a trout so long, broad, and thick as to outbulk anything in an angler's wildest dream. Barely perceptible in the wine-colored shadows at first, he grew more luminously definite while he lifted, somewhat as if the fluid matrix were giving birth to a stupendous, living jewel, balancing it on fins, and streamlining it for speed. How such a patriarch happened to lurk in so narrow a hideout, or why he had failed to devour all the smaller fry, were mysteries never to be solved.

Common sense declared it impracticable to handle a goodly fish in the thick of that brush, but common sense did not stop me from trying. With pounding pulse I flicked the fly to the spot where he had faded and allowed it to drift across the pool. Almost immediately he boiled beside the feathery sham and then whisked back into the unknown. There was something positively dreamlike in the appearance and disappearance of that regal fish, abrupt and unaccountable as the Cheshire cat in *Alice in Wonderland*. Like that notorious feline, too, the trout simply would not remain in

obscurity, and presently I glimpsed him dawning in the deeps in the same mysterious manner as before. He must have seen me on his initial rise, yet he again steered deliberately toward the lure and rolled a flank as ruddy as Scotch gold.

Until that moment his movement had appeared as sluggish as those of a well-fed carp, but when I pricked him, there was plenty of violent action. His first tremendous flounce carried him into deep water under a root, snarling the line in next to no time; but the hole was so limited that his next convulsion whirled him toward the surface. As the line was now useless, I dropped the rod, seized the leader, and twitched him into an overhanging bush. Had he not been shooting upward, I could never have yanked him clear, for he proved even more huge than I had imagined, broad out of all proportion to his length and correspondingly hefty. For a split second he dangled, while I made a spasmodic effort to net him in midair, but the barb pulled out of his lip before I could touch him. Nor did he plunge alone, as I lost footing and soused into icy water up to my chin. A jay overhead jeered outrageously, and I felt as if I had lost a thousand dollars.

On thinking matters over later, I concluded that it might have been possible to embrace that trout by a flying tackle. The cold bath was inevitable, so that I might as well have had something to show for the immersion. Whether or not tiger tactics might have succeeded where the more conventional method failed, the whole episode seemed absolutely futile, and probably would have been so, no matter what I tried.

I comforted myself with the hope of confiding everything to my companion, who would surely sympathize. To my cha-grin, he smiled rather perfunctorily at the story. "You haven't been dozing and rolled into the brook, have you?" he suggested dryly. "We can't eat that kind of fish, you know. Why not stick to something that I can have for dinner?"

In vain I described the splendors of my trout, his obliging tameness and titanic symmetry. Vehemence provoked only laughter, and eventually the grand old trout became merely one more of those impossible fish which nearly get caught, yet somehow manage to escape. People do not call you a liar in such cases, but they vaguely suggest it, which is infinitely more exasperating to your sporting nature.

Yet, although he meant little to others, that lordly fugitive meant much to me and still does, for that matter. In spite of my failure to secure him, I afterward made him a sort of yardstick by which to gauge the bulk of lesser trout—trout taken by me, needless to say, since it rouses antagonism to apply such airy standards to guerdons won by others. I trust that he still adorns that winy pool in the north woods, waiting for somebody else to try him again. Meanwhile, he sometimes swims into the glow of my camp fire, larger even than when I angled for him.

JUNE 1937

WHY ARTIFICIAL FLIES CATCH TROUT

by EUGENE V. CONNETT III

FOR GENERATIONS anglers have been discovering why trout took artificial flies, and they have presented almost every possible hypothesis. There are those who hold that trout can distinguish color but not form, as opposed to those who believe trout to be color blind but able to distinguish form readily. Many hundreds of anglers, acting upon both theories, have successfully caught trout for years. Another section of our craft say that trout are partially color blind and partially form blind; they think trout will overlook certain minor discrepancies in color and shape, such as a bare hook hanging down from the body of the fly, and will take a fly of sufficiently accurate coloring and shape if they are hungry enough. Still another school maintains that trout can distinguish differences in color tones without actually distinguishing colors themselves. Another class of anglers, on the theory that trout care naught for color except as it affects the silhouette of the fly, strive for density or lack of it, with both color and form, in order that the result may be a fly showing a silhouette such as they imagine the trout might see when gazing at a natural fly. A further theory, which has been most cleverly put into practice, is that the body of the natural fly is translucent and depends on its active coloring, if I may express it that way, for the effect of the light glowing through its body. And finally, an ever-growing class is leaning toward the idea that neither color nor form has anything to do with it, but that the behavior of the artificial fly on the water is all that matters. They do include the importance of size, but feel that almost any fly with enough hackle to make it float high will, when properly handled, catch trout. For the past few years I have leaned strongly to this opinion—and then I happened to watch a goldfish in my aquarium.

In watching my goldfish I was not foolish enough to imagine that any self-re-specting trout would think along the same lines as this brilliant carp; but some of the actions of the latter recalled the times I had watched trout taking their ease when they were entirely unaware of my presence. My goldfish spends most of his waking hours slowly fussing around his little world, sucking in first this and then that, and ninety-eight times out of a hundred spitting it out again. Now, I am quite sure that if I had not been reading Mr. Skues' truly excellent book, *The Way of a Trout with a Fly,* I would have watched that goldfish for many years to come without ever having it direct my mind back to the times I have watched trout fussing around. But Mr. Skues' keenness apparently had stirred my usually sluggish mind to the point where it only needed some sort of object lesson to produce something epochal!

Not once, but many times, I have lain hidden in the grass on the bank of a stream or peered through the holes in a bridge, and during these lazy watches I have seen trout lying in the gentle current, now moving a

fraction of an inch this way, and then an inch that way, merely to examine some small item that happened to float down past them. Sometimes they would take these nondescript objects in their mouths and spit them out again; at other times what went into their mouths was swallowed. Often the trout would come up to the surface and either take objects into their mouths or merely nose at them and sink down to their original position, to await the advent of something else to be examined. I have even thrown little pieces of match sticks out on the water, and have seen them taken into the fishes' mouths only to be rejected. I have been so dastardly as to throw a cigarette butt on the water, and have actually seen it seized by a trout—to be quickly spat out, of course. Once I broke the points off a number of old flies and threw these on the water—one at a time. Although there was no rise of natural fly on, the trout rose to every one of these, often holding them in their mouths for an appreciable time before rejecting them. In this propensity on the part of trout to examine all that which comes within their convenient range I believe lies the true explanation of why they will take an artificial fly—almost regardless of what the theory of its design may have been.

Now, I realize that trout do not always appear to be in the quiet, exploratory moods in which I have watched them try out whatever came their way. Nevertheless, by retaining certain of the items they took into their mouths they showed that they were feeding, or willing to feed. At none of the times I watched such trout was there a good hatch of flies on the water—else I should have probably been fishing for, rather than watching, them. But what an easy step it is now for us to imagine a hatch of flies on or under the surface. The first nymphs begin to appear and, instead of being rejected, are swallowed. This may even arouse still more the curiosity to test what comes along. Finally, flies float down on the surface, are tried out, and are swallowed.

It may be possible that there is something more attractive in a fly on the surface than there is in a nymph under it; there probably is, if we can believe the evidence of our eyes during a good rise of flies. I should not be surprised if, after the first half-dozen olive duns have been tried and not found wanting, a distinct appetite for this species of insect was aroused in the trout. He may say to himself: "These floating objects, which more or less resemble each other, first because their feet all make little indentations in the surface while still outside of my window, and then because they move along exactly at the same speed as I look up at them out in the air above me

while floating in my window, all taste good. My attention is now caught by them coming along on the surface, and therefore I won't bother with those little odds and ends that are floating along underneath." Then he may say to himself, "Huh! look at that bally thing hanging down from that floating object over there! Looks a bit more substantial than these others. Hello! There's another one! Might as well try it out." And to his sorrow he cannot spit it out.

That almost everything, including natural flies, is examined in the mouth before being swallowed, is, I think, a safe assumption; otherwise we should hook more trout in the throat than we do. An old trout, experienced through many seasons of feeding on insects, may become so expert in distinguishing objects that after he is fairly under way during a hatch he will gulp flies down without much trying out. Such a fish may distinguish size, behavior, shape, and color to an unusual degree, and therefore be content to feed on just one class of object at a time—probably the most plentiful at the moment. That he is willing to try out some other object now and then most of us have had the good fortune to discover.

It may be asked why trout will not at all times try out almost everything that comes their way. The answer may be made, because of fear—fear of other fish, animals, birds, anglers, disturbance of the water, vibrations on the banks, and the like; because of certain depressions, probably caused by temperature of water or air or by barometric pressures; and, more rarely, because of surfeit. But, generally speaking, I believe that trout will try out objects most of the time, unless there is a definite external influence, such as I have mentioned, causing them to refrain from doing so. There must be infinitesimal drags, of which the angler is not conscious, that warn a trout not to try out an artificial fly; there are certain appearances of the leader which warn an experienced trout to leave some artificials alone—in spite of the fact that he may be tempted to examine them. Certainly, young and inexperienced trout will rush at a fly when an older one will not come near it, which furnishes us with sufficient cause for believing that trout do learn by experience.

Lest I be accused of trying to beg the question, I must give further consideration to where a trout draws the line regarding what shall be tried out in the mouth and what shall be tried out by external examination. The line is undoubtedly not a fixed one. The prevalence of any one sort of food will play its part, as well as the prevalence of food in general. The trout which took my cigarette butt in his mouth on Wednesday might have refused to do so on Tuesday or on Thursday. The trout which took my Olive Dun in his mouth on Tuesday might well have refused to do so on Monday, especially if there was a hatch of olives when he took it and there were no flies out when he refused it. Now, there is more resemblance between an artificial Olive Dun, including its hook, and a natural olive dun, than there is between a cigarette butt and a natural olive dun. There is more resemblance to the real olive dun in the artificial one floating naturally, without drag and with leader away from the trout, than there is in the artificial dragging over the surface. There is more resemblance to the natural in an Olive Dun of the same size than there is in one two inches long and two inches high. If we are willing to admit that trout learn by experience, we should be willing to admit that experience will help them to draw the line somewhere as regards what they should and what they should not try out in the mouth. Somewhere in between the cigarette butt, the dragging artificial, the two-inch artificial, and the free-floating, approximately life-sized artificial, each individual trout will draw his individual line. If he is at peace with the world, unworried by danger, unaffected by temperature and pressure, he will draw his line with less discrimination. If anglers have bothered him, vermin worried him, weather upset him, perhaps he will not take even naturals.

So far we have considered only such objects as float down in or on the water to the trout. There is, of course, another class, comprising minnows, insects which have the power of self-propulsion, and other objects that may move against or across the current of the stream. Some excellently expressed theories concerning the irritability of the nerves of the trout have been brought forward to explain their seizing this type of objects. Why cause the poor trout's nerves to tingle and jump just because of the direction in which the object is moving? What could be more natural than the fact that a trout will put more vim into seizing an object that is moving away from him than one which is quietly coming toward him? It should not take a trout long to discover that such an object cannot be examined in the mouth unless he moves after it. And in the case of these objects, he draws his line just as he does in the case of those that come to him quietly, or those that are stationary.

To sum up: It is a natural instinct with trout to examine objects with a view to discovering whether they are fit for food, either by trying them out in their mouths or by nosing them, perhaps looking at them closely, or even smelling them. Some objects, under certain conditions, are taken into the mouth; others are not. The trout draws a line somewhere regarding which are to be taken into his mouth and which are not. This line is affected by a great many external conditions. However, the instinct is always there to examine the object, and external conditions or experience determine whether the instinct is to be overruled or not.

In the case of artificial dry flies, their action on the water is probably the only attribute we as anglers can control, as no imitation has ever been exact in any other respect than action. So long as we can control this one thing, we should subordinate as far as may be necessary the other attributes of a fly in order to permit us to secure the highest degree of control of action. If action is perfect, it will influence the point at which a trout will draw his line as regards trying out the fly in his mouth. Next to action, we can control size; and this should be considered as the second most desirable attribute.

Our definite knowledge of how color, as we see it, appears to the trout is so hypothetical at this time that its value is questionable. Mr. Dunne's theories are probably the most practical, as they concern floating artificials. Therefore, we should not strive for color beyond the point where it may in the slightest degree affect action or size. Shape appears to be the least important attribute of an artificial fly in determining the line at which the trout will decide to

try out the fly in his mouth; the cigarette butt plus our own experience with Palmer Hackles and other "shapeless" flies bears out this statement fully. I therefore consider that action, size, shape, and color all play their part in the construction of the most useful trout flies, but I do not think that action should be sacrificed for shape and color—at least, until such time as we can say, "This is beyond peradventure how a trout views color and shape," which we certainly cannot say at this time.

The action of a trout fly on the surface includes all those things we would put under the name of behavior. A fly floats—only too seldom!—without the least suspicion of a drag; it floats on the tips of its hackles, just as a natural floats on its "feet." If, in order to make its color apparent, we make the fly so that it floats with its body, instead of its hackle tips, on the surface, we have sacrificed action for color. If we make a fly of such a color that we cannot see it distinctly on the water, we shall probably have sacrificed action for size, for this almost invisible fly will drag before we are aware of it—in fact, it may drag throughout its entire course without our being aware of it. There are degrees of sacrifice, and common sense must temper the whole matter.

JULY 1928

DRY-FLY MANIA

by JOHN ALDEN KNIGHT JR.

A FEW YEARS ago I attended a dinner given by one of the sportsmen's clubs in the metropolitan area. One of the speakers of the evening made this remark—based his talk on it, for that matter.

"Gentlemen," he said. "You may use wet flies, bucktails, streamers, and nymphs, if you choose. For my part, I'll stick to the rules of the game; I'll take them dry or not at all."

A lot of men applauded. And I, feeling uncomfortably out of tune with both the statement and its reception, sat and wondered at the irresistible power of ballyhoo. These men were—and are—intelligent men. They occupy places in the sun, run their own businesses, and live handsomely. Yet they applauded this bit of banality as though it had been a veritable pearl of wisdom that had been tossed among us.

The dry or floating fly has been in use for a great many years, not only in England but in this country as well. Books on angling show us that as far back as the early nineties and, possibly, earlier, anglers carried with them a small bottle of liquid paraffin or kerosene with which they dressed their wet flies so as to make them float when the occasion demanded. Gradually the method grew more popular. Flies came to be no longer just trout flies. They were divided into two classes, sinking flies and floating flies. The next step was the publishing of two books on the subject of dry-fly fishing. These came on the market in rapid succession and were the first American works dealing with the use of the dry fly. Then came the deluge.

Angling writers, always on the lookout for new material, took up the discussion of the dry fly in the outdoor magazines. Great

mystery was built around its use and a "dry-fly man" was regarded with awe by the run-of-the-mine anglers. "Drag" was held up before us as the angler's curse, and admonitions came from all sides, cautioning us against "drag" and its dire consequences. Much stress was placed upon the ability to throw the right and left loop. Many hours and millions of words were wasted in the old "wet-fly–dry-fly" controversy. Then, out of this confusion, emerged a group of individuals who inevitably gravitated together in forming the informal, but none the less decisive, cult of purism.

The early stages of dry-fly purism were no doubt a lot of fun; the variations in tackle, the endless discussions of line and leader tapers, the constant purchasing of new equipment (which entails that ever-delightful pastime of hanging around the tackle stores and talking about fishing). Undoubtedly, this new toy of dry-fly fishing was a great boon for both anglers and tackle dealers. The results, as we see them today, in improved rods, lines, reels, flies, and leaders were, of course, well worth the effort expended. But the mystery which surrounds any new development must be dispersed eventually. The groundwork having been done and the results being well established, let us take a look at dry-fly fishing as we now have it.

In the first place, dry-fly fishing is, to my mind at least, the simplest and pleas-antest of our current methods of taking trout. Equipped with a dry-fly rod, a tapered line and leader, and some bivisibles or spiders, any angler, who is possessed of the barest fundamentals of casting and fishing knowledge, can reasonably expect to have a fair day's sport on a stream which holds even the average amount of trout. The dry fly has reduced his difficulties from three to two dimensions. It will be difficult for him to make a bad cast with a bivisible or a spider fly, and he can see plainly everything that goes on. His casting may be faulty and badly executed, but, if he is using a fuzzy fly, the results he gets will be out of all proportion to his ability. Timing may remain an unknown quantity. All in all, Mr. Dab is now in much better shape for taking trout than he was before the development of the dry fly.

Please do not make the mistake of believing that I was immune from dry-fly mania. I used to adopt my best holier-than-thou manner and talk with a raised eyebrow to those inept creatures who still persisted in the use of the wet fly. I don't think I ever reached the purist stage, but I was pretty bad, just the same. Then one day I went fishing in the Little Mongaup at De Bruce, New York.

I had walked up the road beside the stream to a point about a mile from the inn and was just entering the water when I spied a man, evidently a farmer, sitting on the opposite bank rigging up his tackle. His wading equipment consisted of short rubber boots which reached to his knees. His rod was a lancewood affair with buggy-whip action. His line was a cheap, enameled one, wound on a tiny brass reel which might have cost fifty cents originally but which had long since lost its tackle-store gloss. As I passed the time of day with him, he took from his pocket a leader, still dry and tightly coiled, and placed it in the water where he held it down with his foot. Then, opening his battered fly envelope, he took out, after a certain amount of rummaging, three large snelled flies of nondescript pattern. These he held in his mouth while he uncoiled his half-soaked leader and fastened it to his line with a bow knot. When new, it probably was six feet long, but it had seen better days.

Suppressing a smile, I moved upstream and began the afternoon's fishing, secure in my knowledge of dry-fly methods and feeling somewhat sorry for the farmer. The trout were singularly unresponsive to my offerings, and, after an hour's casting had been rewarded by only two small fish, I sat down on the bank, leaned my rod against a tree, and lighted a cigarette. As I sat there my farmer friend came into sight. He had been fishing upstream not a hundred yards behind me. Using a short line, he covered every inch of the stream, as he slowly made his way toward me, being careful not to

step into water too deep for his knee-length boots. As I watched him, he expertly extracted a fine trout from under a rock to which I had given only passing attention. Well, I thought, accidents will happen.

As he came abreast of me, I inquired as to his luck. Without replying he opened his time-worn creel and displayed a mess of trout that would make any angler envious. Right then and there I decided that I had a lot to learn about trout fishing. Respectfully, I asked his permission to watch him fish for awhile. He accepted this tribute with modesty and good-naturedly assented. Accordingly, I unjointed my rod, and the balance of the afternoon was spent in absorbing wet-fly information which has proved invaluable in later years. At broken-water pocket fishing I have never seen his equal.

Although it was a severe jolt to my ego, I have always been grateful to this man. Through his kindly influence, I learned a lesson which some men refuse to learn— two lessons in fact. Not only did I absorb many of the finer points in the use of the wet fly, but also did I have impressed upon me the futility of adhering to one method when that method was not indicated under a given set of conditions.

The habit of using a dry fly to the exclusion of all else is an easy one to acquire. A well-cast dry fly is a tempting-looking offering, as it bobs its way down the surface of a wavy, fast-water run. The handling and casting of it will, of itself, impart a great deal of satisfaction to the angler regardless of results. It is my feeling that this sense of satisfaction is what keeps many men from changing to other methods when the trout are not surface feeding. Again, it may be the fact that fishing is a relaxing, lazy pastime. It has a lulling effect on the perceptions of the average angler, which makes him overlook the obvious solution of his failure to take trout, while he continues his fruitless efforts with the dry fly. Two of the more common conditions under which the use of the dry fly is next to hopeless are those times when the trout are bottom feeding, tails up and noses among rocks, and when they are bulging to rising nymphs. The number of wasted hours which the average dry-fly purist will spend in fruitless casting when either of these conditions maintain is beyond comprehension.

Two seasons ago, a man who is not only an enthusiastic sportsman, but who, in addition, makes sports his business, took three or four fine trout from a famous pool on the Ausable one morning. He returned to the pool that afternoon and found the trout rising throughout its entire length. Using the same dry fly which had taken his fish that morning, he spent over three hours in dry-fly casting without getting so much as a single rise to his fly. He did not consider important the fact that there were no duns floating at the time. Neither did he make any serious effort to learn what the trout were taking. Instead, he stood and cast a Light Cahill over several dozen bulging fish. By watching the water and identifying the nymph which was drifting at the time and then matching that nymph, he stood a fair chance of a wonderful afternoon's fishing. Instead, he elected to "stick to the rules of the game and take them dry—or not at all."

Last spring, I sat on the bank of a favorite pool on the East Branch of the Delaware. Below me was a dry-fly fisherman, laboring mightily as he made his way upstream casting, casting his floater regardless of the fact that not a fish was moving. After he had quit the pool, I walked to the riffle at its head and, using a long line and letting a small wet fly drag slowly over the rocks on the bottom, I hooked four fish, one of them a very heavy trout. The ba-rometer had been falling slowly since morning, and the trout were in hiding under the rocks and ledges on the bottom. A fly pulled past their noses would tempt them, but a floating fly had no appeal whatever.

It has been said about a certain bridge expert and his wife that the cause of their phenomenal success is due to the fact that their opponents always play a system, while they, on the other hand, play bridge. By the same token, a purist adheres to a method, the rules of which are all carefully laid out for him. On the other hand, an angler—in the true sense of the word—takes his gear and goes fishing, mindful of and prepared to meet any particular set of conditions with which he is confronted. His stream thermometer and his barometer will tell him pretty closely just what behavior to expect on the part of the fish. His analytical, or "fish," sense will show him the method to use or not to use. In other words, he doesn't go dry-fly fishing; he goes trout fishing. There is a vast difference.

Despite the foregoing, I'm not unmindful that the purist has his uses. He is a valuable member of the community, and I'm grateful to him. He's a double-barreled conservationist. Not only does he lend his enthusiastic aid to the restocking problem, but also he does relatively little damage since, as a rule, he takes fewer fish than he would were his scope widened. He.is a staunch and loyal member of his angling club. He keeps the tackle dealers busy supplying him with the best in dry-fly equipment, and his undying enthusiasm usually makes him good company. So—as I say—he has his uses, and it is my hope that the clan may never diminish.

MARCH 1937

JACK RUSSELL will long be remembered for his book *Jack and I and The Salmon*, and for his camp on the Miramichi in New Brunswick. The high cost of salmon leases—even in the 1930s—gives one pause, but you should know that Russell's old salmon camp has been purchased and is still open to the public, albeit for a price.

SALMON FISHING ON THE MIRAMICHI

CHANGED CONDITIONS OPEN THE RIVERS
OF NEW BRUNSWICK TO AMERICAN ANGLERS

by JACK RUSSELL

THE ICE has gone out of the rivers in New Brunswick, the weeks of waiting are over in the cities, and the guides are out with their sportsmen. It is the season of the kelt—salmon as he is known at this time of the year—and he starts down the river from his spawning ground pointing the way to the year-old parr, or baby salmon, who is going to the sea for the first time.

There is an angler casting at the head of a well-known pool on the Miramichi. The river is just right; conditions are ideal. The guide, standing in the stern, holds the canoe steady with his pole, and indicates the spot for the fisherman to start casting. His fly is placed with care. A mighty splash

and a salmon is well hooked. Downstream he goes, taking out yards of line from the screaming reel, bending the rod nearly double; the first fish of the season is on. Again and again the fish leaps into the air. The guide slowly poles the canoe ashore where the fight continues on more equal terms. With the angler on the land the battle moves downstream, for there is no holding that leaping, charging opponent on the other end of the line. The guide follows, net in hand, ready for the finishing touch. The rapids at the end of the pool spell defeat for the man and freedom for the fish. He must be stopped before reaching white water. At the mouth of a spring brook the final stand is made. The fish sulks in a deep hole. Relentlessly the bowed rod has its way, and after twenty minutes, slowly but surely the salmon is brought to the net. A moment of exaltation and the guide is instructed to let him go. "Probably we will get him another time."

More money is spent in taking the Atlantic salmon, the best and most widely known of all game fish, than any other species. A river like the Restigouche, for instance, brings an annual rental of $75,500 for the exclusive privilege of fishing it, and the mere fact of having a lease or ownership of one of these fine salmon rivers does not necessarily mean that the water is fished all the time, either, as I know of controlled waters that go through the best part of the season without being fished.

Each year a greater interest is shown in angling for salmon. There are more articles than ever on the salmon, his life and his habits; and as the provincial government realizes the tremendous value of the tourist business, it is giving more consideration to the conservation and propagation of its fisheries. The American public is fast learning to play, and it is reasonable to expect a larger number of fishermen on the rivers each year.

Most of the rivers of New Brunswick have been closed to the public on account of being privately owned or leased, and on those rivers that have been open for fishing the accommodations for the class of angler who could afford this sport have been very limited. This condition, however, has been met by the outfitters of New Brunswick. They have built camps that offer much comfort and eliminate all the hardships, and these establishments, located on the so-called open waters, like the famous Miramichi, are attracting new groups of sportsmen. Up to a short time ago the angler who could dissertate on salmon experiences was listened to respectfully by his fellow men, but the advent of good roads, a newborn desire to get far afield, and the lower cost of equipment have brought about a changed condition. Salmon anglers have discovered these open waters.

The life of the salmon is full of interest. He goes to the sea, after a year or fifteen months, from the upper part of the river in which he was spawned, and comes back when he is two or three years old, as a grilse, weighing from three to six pounds, and spawns for the first time. During the time the grilse is in the sea he takes on weight at an unprecedented rate, frequently gaining several pounds in a few months. After a winter in fresh water he goes back to the sea again as a kelt, and finally returns as a full-fledged or bright salmon that, according to his feeding in salt water, will weigh up to thirty-five or forty pounds, and offer the last word in angling.

When the fish goes out in the spring he

❧ SALMON FISHING ON THE MIRAMICHI ❧

117

is lean and racy and strikes a fly easily, but after a season of feeding in the sea he returns very much heavier and not so easily interested in a lure. It is a well-known fact that he does not eat anything while in fresh water, for if a fish is opened at this time nothing is found in his stomach, and nobody knows why he takes a fly, but he will rise to one the same as a feeding trout.

When he is in condition to return to fresh water he has a long, hard battle for existence. The commercial fisheries with their nets at the mouth of the rivers are his first menace, and if he is fortunate enough to elude capture there, he has the rips and rapids of the river to negotiate. On reaching the pool at the end of one of these rushes upstream the fish will lie in quiet water and rest, and it is here that the angler seeks him out. He will lie in one place for hours at a time, and it would seem that he travels only at night. I have frequently spotted fishes early in the morning that would stay in the same pool all day. Toward evening, however, they would show signs of restlessness, leaping clear of the water, and finally moving off upstream during the night. I have also seen marked fish stay in one pool for several days. When the fish come into the river early in the summer it is doubtful if they stay to spawn, but when they come during the fall it is for spawning purposes only.

During May the salmon is easily taken on a fly, and although there has been some criticism on taking the fish during this season, government regulations in New Brunswick allow the killing of but one fish a day, so the species is but little affected by the spring fishing.

You may cast all day over several salmon and never get a rise, and yet you may take the only fish in a pool on the first cast. It frequently happens that a fish may have had a perfectly cast fly of a certain pattern drop right over him several times without even noticing it, and then he will rush at it on the next cast.

The various patterns of salmon flies are well-nigh inexhaustible because they do not in any way resemble the native insects as do trout flies. It is remarkable that salmon will take a fly at all, as it is not their natural food. There are so many combinations of colors and designs of salmon flies that it is impossible to name them all. There are a few standard wet flies, such as Jock Scott, Black Dose, Brown Fairy, Silver Wilkinson, Durham Ranger, and Silver Doctor, which are used by nearly all salmon anglers, and if their fishing is extended to the use of the dry fly the Colonel Monell, Soldier Palmer, Pink Lady, and Gray Palmer are the most commonly used.

The expert can kill the largest fish on a number 10 or number 12 fly, but the average angler generally uses a number 6 or number 8 double hook with the wet fly, and, as a rule, the number 6 single hook with the dry fly. In European waters a spinning bait is sometimes used, but in New Brunswick waters the fly only is legal. This makes for sportsmanship in every sense of the word, as salmon are not feeding in fresh water and everything depends on their mood, not their appetite.

The grilse can be taken with a light rod and small fly. I frequently take a grilse with a 6¼-ounce rod and a number 12 dry fly, and this combination gives one a thrill little exceeded by a heavier fish on bigger tackle.

When salmon angling was first introduced into America we used the long, heavy, two-handed rods of English manufacture, but as we became more familiar with conditions, there was evolved a lighter and more easily handled rod for heavy fishing, and it is not an unusual thing to see the light single-handed rod killing full-grown fish. These light salmon rods, however, are little used abroad and are catalogued by English rod makers as for use by American anglers only.

If the angler is using a canoe he is dependent, to a large extent, on the skill of his guide. These rivermen seem to be a part of their surroundings. They are generally very good fishermen themselves, know their waters, and can spot a fish like a hawk. When it comes to handling a canoe in fast water they have no superiors, and are, apparently, tireless when poling a canoe or a boat upstream.

When taking a long canoe trip down the river from Deersdale, which is almost the headwaters of the Miramichi, the angler comes through a wilderness of green, timbered hills and granite cliffs. There is a new pool to be fished every little while, and numerous trout brooks which keep the pan well supplied with breakfasts.

After passing through miles of unsettled country the river widens out, the first of the upper settlements is reached, and the thin wisp of smoke from the cookhouse of the base camp, sitting high up on the bank among the spruce trees, reminds you that the journey is about over. There is hope that you will take a big fish at the last minute to bring home; there are plans to return the next year; and there is the wish that the remark of the late Fred Buckland, English sportsman, might come true. Mr. Buckland declared that salmon always returned to the place of their birth, and added that he would like to hatch them out by the thousands in his own kitchen.

MAY 1930

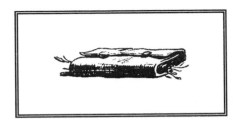

TROUT FISHING IN PONDS AND LAKES

by EDWARD R. HEWITT

THE MAN who is a past master in brook fishing and knows all there is on this subject is often lost when it comes to fishing ponds or lakes for trout. The conditions are so different that his stream methods and often his tackle and flies are almost useless. He goes home feeling that trout only show good sport in running waters. He would feel quite differently if he knew the game better.

The insect life in still water is of quite a different character from that in streams, and the habits of trout of course vary with their food. Also the varieties of trout behave quite differently from each other in still waters while in streams their behavior is not at all so unlike. Let us take them up in order and see what is the usual course of things.

Brook trout rise to the surface feeding on insects just as soon as the ice leaves the lakes and continue to feed on the surface as long as the surface water is cool and the supply of food abundant. When the top waters begin to get warm they seek the lower levels where it is cooler and where they find more food. If there are spring holes where fresh water comes in, they are sure to be found there in the later season while the rest of the water is likely to be bare of these fish. Such conditions are usual in all northern lakes I have seen. Brook trout come to the surface at times and will take a fly even in the warm weather if there happens to be an insect hatch. As the surface waters cool off to a considerable extent at night, they are likely to come up late at night, and the best time to get them in warm weather on a fly is at daylight when the night insects are still on

the surface and the water is cool. I have often had good fishing at daylight in warm weather when everyone said that trout were through coming to the top for the season. The worst time to fish for them in hot weather is in the evening, because then the water is at its warmest for the whole twenty-four hours. Yet most fishermen look forward to the evening fishing and wonder why they come home with little or nothing.

Brook trout can be caught in lakes or ponds almost any time of the season by fishing below the surface and usually near the bottom. This can be done with flies with some chance of getting some, but is far more successful with bait or with a small spinner or a spinner and bait. This is not a very sporting way to fish, but at times it is the only way trout can be caught.

Brown trout in this country have no-where been a successful lake or pond fish. No one seems to know the reason for this. They grow well and reach great size, yet they are rarely caught either on flies or on bait. There are a few lakes I know where there is a short season of fair fly-fishing for brown trout, but these lakes are exceptional. I have tried for them in every way with flies and bait and spinners and failed to make good catches. The best results have always been with an Archer Spinner and a minnow, but I dislike this kind of fishing and never do it except to find out whether fish are present. I have speared brown trout at night, up to fourteen pounds, mistaking them for carp, and they must have been fairly numerous in the water, but no one ever caught any. My friend Mr. Rogers had a lake near Poughkeepsie which was full of large brown trout and he never succeeded in catching one of them.

These fish behave quite differently all over Europe. In Scotland the fly-fishing in the lochs is excellent all the season. In fact, some of these waters provide the best still-water fly-fishing I have ever seen. In Loch Leven, which is considered the best fly-fishing lake in the British Isles, the trout seem to feed mostly on midge larvae which come up continually from the bottom. The trout follow them up and are always to be found near the surface, where they take flies readily. This lake occupies about 1,200 acres and they regularly catch about 50,000 trout each season which total up to 40,000 pounds. This has been going on for a great many years with no reduction of the catch. We have no similar lake in this country that I have heard of. I wish someone would find

out why brown trout in lakes are not good fly-fishing fish in this country. So far I have seen no explanation of it.

Rainbow trout seem to be the best lake fish of the trout family for our country. At least they are more often successful than brook trout for lake fishing. They seem not to mind the warmer water near the surface and will take a fly over a longer season than brook trout. They also seem to make a more rapid growth in lakes and are better able to look after themselves against predacious fish. I know of several lakes inhabited by black bass and pickerel in which they have been very successful and have furnished good fishing. This is almost never the case with brook trout.

Rainbows have one marked peculiarity which anyone intending to stock with them should know. They resemble salmon in the fact that they have light scales like the salmon parr until they reach about eight inches long. Then they seem to turn silvery and their scales get firmer. It has been clearly shown that in lakes they must go to deep water and not remain around the shores when they are small or they will be destroyed by the predacious fish. They cannot go to deep water until they get their silvery scales, as they cannot stand the pressure. It is necessary then to put them out in lakes always ten inches long or longer if they are to succeed. This was worked out by Mr. Kyle at Tuxedo a number of years ago after they had had poor results in stocking with steelheads for several years. He put small fish in wire cages and lowered them to different levels in the water and found that the small fish could not stand a depth of more than ten feet of water. This evidently was not deep enough for them to escape their enemies. As soon as fish ten inches in length or longer were put out, the stocking became a success. I would always recommend rainbows for lake or pond stocking in preference to brook trout if the outlet can be screened so that they cannot get out. If they can, they will largely seek salt water. Rainbows seem to thrive on lake foods and make far better growth than brook trout in still waters.

I am often asked how one should fish with a fly in lakes, as there is no current to draw the fly. Certainly lake fishing with a fly is quite a different art from brook fishing, and the man who is successful in a stream may be a complete failure in a lake.

There are a number of tricks I have found useful in the tackle. Long leaders I regard as an absolute necessity in catching shy fish in still waters, and fine leaders as well. I use a leader of at least twelve feet in length with the last four feet next the fly not over .006 inch in diameter. My patent opaque stained leaders are far better for still-water fishing than any other stained leader, and of course I always use them.

There are several ways of using the fly which are successful. In Europe they nearly always use wet flies and draw them slowly on top or just below the surface. They generally use two or more flies and make the droppers just touch the water surface, and often jiggle them so as to make little light flashes below the surface. This method of fishing is regarded as the most practical and successful for lakes and is almost the universal rule. Flies are selected suitable to the waters to be fished. They do not necessarily resemble the insects found in the water, and in fact few of the best Scotch loch flies have any resemblance to any insects I know. They seem to attract by their motion and light flashes on the surface more than by their imitation of insect life. It is found, however, that they must be of the right size for the particular water being fished. They should correspond to the insects present in size, if not in color and appearance.

Flies resembling small minnows such as bucktails and streamers are of course very successful in waters where fish feed largely on minnows. They should always be tried. In fishing them use only one fly at a time. They work far better in the water in this way.

There are two other ways of fishing lakes in which I have been singularly successful and which are not usually practiced by anglers.

The dry fly can be used with deadly effect when fish are feeding at the surface, and at times they will bring up trout from deep water, as the following instance will show.

The Duke of Athol very kindly sent me permission to fish his own private lake, Loch Ordie, which is considered one of the best in Scotland and rarely fished by anyone but himself. It happened to be a bright day and I reached the loch about noon with an English friend who was stopping with me. The gillie informed us that the fishing would be poor until evening and that it was small use to go out on the water until later. However, we pushed off, and my friend put on the regular loch flies they always use. Realizing that they would be of little use in the middle of the day, I tied on a large spider dry fly of the Brown Bivisible pattern and oiled it and cast it out as far as I could and let it sit on the water perfectly still for a moment and then gave it a little twitch. The purpose of this was to attract the attention of any fish which had seen the fly alight and had his eye on it. The motion of the fly simulates an insect about to rise, and the impulse to rush and get it before it gets away is often irresistible to a trout.

After I had made a few of these casts, the gillie remarked that it was no use fishing with that feather duster, it would scare every trout in the lake. I said it might, but my friend was not doing much with his loch flies. Just then the lake exploded and a large trout leaped in the air with my fly in his mouth. He had been down deep and came fast and could not stop. He was hooked easily and played and landed. He weighed just three pounds. The gillie remarked, "That was a marvelous accident." Well, out went the duster again and in a little while another explosion. After three or four of these my friend turned around and asked if I had any more of these dusters. Well, he soon got used to the method and we kept catching these large fish every few minutes, some even larger than the first. I looked in the bottom of the boat and saw we had enough, seventeen as I remember, so we rowed back. I did not wish to abuse the Duke's hospitality.

Next day I wrote him a note and sent him some of the flies. Later he wrote that he could raise the fish but could not hook any, so I guess the lake is safe until I go to Scotland again. I wonder if the gillie has recovered yet.

This same method can be practiced with small dry flies down to number 20 midges, which are often very effective in lakes when small flies are on the surface. They are used in the same way and allowed to remain still and then slightly moved to make a flash. I have rarely failed to catch fish in lakes by this method even when they were very difficult to get.

The last method I use is nymph-fishing. There are many lakes where trout rarely take flies on the surface but feed almost entirely on nymphs often well below the top. In order to get these fish we must find out what size and color of nymph they are feeding on, because trout will rarely take nymphs very different from their regular food. They can see the nymph clearly below the surface and they don't like anything abnormal. One can find the right nymph by opening a trout if one has been caught, or, if not, must see what is in the water. If you can't find anything, then experiment with everything in the box.

Trout take nymphs in two ways: either when they are pulled through the water at just the right speed or when they are allowed to sink after the cast and slowly pulled toward the surface. So that the leader may sink readily, grease the line and leader up to about four feet from the fly; then suck the balance of the leader in the mouth or rub it with some glycerine and water. Cast the nymph out and let it sink and then pull very slowly. The fly will rise to the surface simulating an insect rising. The trout generally takes it just as it reaches the surface. I have seen trout come twenty feet for a nymph fished in this way. I use nymphs from number 18 hooks to number 3. These sizes seem to cover the sizes of the nymphs generally found in lakes. Where there are May-fly hatches larger nymphs must be used, of course, as the nymph of the May fly is nearly an inch long.

Flying ants are often useful in lake fishing, especially when they are being blown on the water in numbers from the land.

There is no reason to give up on lake fishing and think that the trout cannot be caught. All methods of fishing should first be tried.

APRIL 1935

AND SO IT GOES

IN FLY-FISHING TECHNICAL SKILL ALONE WILL NOT

BRING A FULL CREEL, BUT MUST BE BACKED UP

BY YEARS OF STREAM EXPERIENCE,

ESPECIALLY ON HEAVILY FISHED TROUT WATERS

by EUGENE V. CONNETT III

SEVERAL YEARS ago I went fishing with a friend who had made an excellent reputation for himself as a successful fly-fisherman during the six years since he had taken up the sport. He was a man of unusual attainments, and I had always believed would become a really great fly-fisher if he continued to apply himself to the fine points of the game.

On the day I speak of, conditions were not very propitious—in fact, the water was high, the air cold, and no hatch present. We therefore used wet flies.

In something less than an hour my friend came downstream to where I was enjoying myself, and in marked disgust suggested we leave the stream and seek another with some fish in it. I was somewhat surprised, as I had seven trout in my basket, and I told my friend that this was as good a stream as I knew of within a reasonable distance of where we were.

His surprise at the fact I had seven fish was almost funny. If he should ever see these lines, I know he will not object to my telling the story, for I had undergone an exactly similar experience some years before with my friend George La Branche—and it was one of the most valuable lessons I ever learned in connection with fishing. Briefly, in those days I thought I knew as much as La Branche, he having fished for twice as many years as I! And so my friend had been convinced that

127

although I had fished for twice as many years as he had, nevertheless his skill was such that it must make up for his lack of stream experience.

Having seen my seven fish, looked at the stretch of water from which they had been taken, and examined the fly which took them, my friend did just what I had done some years earlier. He intimated that I knew a lot more than he did about catching trout and asked me to take him in hand. I had been waiting for this opportunity, and willingly accepted the role of tutor, in a most friendly spirit.

Rather than step into the stream myself and deliver a somewhat useless lecture on how to catch trout, I suggested that we walk down to an undisturbed pool below us, and that he fish it in his most skillful manner, while I watched for mistakes. The first one was not long in coming.

Fishing wet, he started in the run at the head of the pool, and did so by stepping into the stream about nine feet above the most likely lie for a good trout. Before he had even made his first cast, I requested him to leave the water and sit down beside me—much to his annoyance. However, he was a sportsman and took his medicine like a man: when he sat beside me I asked him,

"Where is the best spot in that run for a good fish to lie?"

After looking the water over with care, he pointed to a certain rock.

"If you wanted to frighten the fish lying in front of that rock, where would you enter the stream?" I inquired.

"Just where I went in," he replied, in some surprise.

Then I asked him to fish the lower part of the run, down to where it spread out into the pool. With commendable forethought, he took stock of the water before wading into the stream, and when he did enter it he was close to the bank, well above where his fly would be fished, and instead of standing up straight, was kneeling on a rock and using a side cast to keep his rod down. He cast his fly nicely to the far side of the run and let it sweep down across the current, lengthening his line until his fly had covered almost all the water. Each of his casts had been clean-looking, with a tight, straight line. When he was through I suggested that he back out from the water carefully and let me have a try.

On the far side of the stream was a rock, about two feet from the bank, with a branch hanging out over the water which ran along the bank, and I felt that a fish would be lying on the inshore side of the rock, enjoying the protection afforded by the situation. In order to interest this fish, it was necessary to drift the wet fly down between the rock and the shore, under the overhanging branch—not a very difficult thing to do, if one employed a curve cast to the left, with plenty of slack line on the

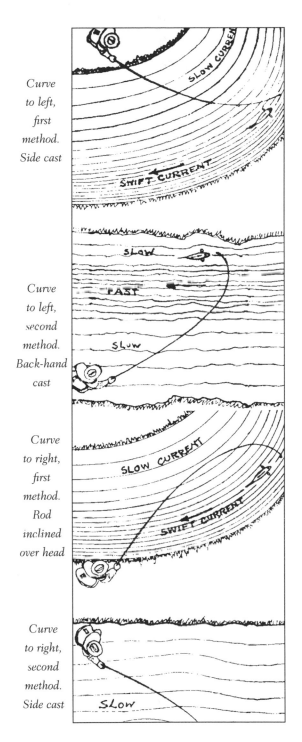

Curve to left, first method. Side cast

Curve to left, second method. Back-hand cast

Curve to right, first method. Rod inclined over head

Curve to right, second method. Side cast

water. The second cast rose the fish, and my friend was a trifle annoyed, as he could not see why his fly had not taken this fish as it swung past that rock on the offshore side. From where he was sitting he could not see my fly, and therefore did not realize exactly what had happened. When I joined him on the bank, I explained it, telling him why I thought the fish would be on the inshore side of the rock, pointing out the excellent protection from winged enemies afforded by the branch, and the satisfactory feeding possibilities of the current. I also showed him a piece of old leader tangled in the branch, where some other fisherman had got himself into trouble at some time.

My friend agreed it was a perfect lie for a fish. I asked him why he didn't think of that before he started to fish the easy open water which every other angler who had fished the run ahead of him had carefully covered.

This little lesson resulted in a half hour of learning the curve casts—and any reasonably efficient caster can learn them in half an hour, although he will have to practice a lot longer than that to achieve real accuracy.

My friend was then asked to fish the pool itself, a large, quiet expanse of water, fairly deep along the far bank, with patches of rhododendron hanging out over the water here and there. It was a long cast across to that inviting bank, which was the only place a fish would lie during the day.

My friend stepped gingerly into the calm water and began working out his fly toward the first patch of rhododendron, under which a fish was undoubtedly lying—probably a good fish, too. When the fly was ten feet from its mark, it fouled some branches behind my friend on the next back cast. This elicited several highly justified cuss words, and when I had freed the fly, he waded out several feet farther into the pool, sending a series of waves rippling across its surface to the far bank— thus notifying the trout that someone was in the pool, and arousing its instinct for self-preservation to a point where its instinct to feed was entirely submerged.

After ten minutes of futile casting, I remarked that while patience might be a great virtue in the art of catching trout, it should be applied at the proper part of the proceedings, and suggested that my friend take a rest with me on the bank. I explained to him that the longer he continued to drop his fly near the fish, the more convinced the fish would probably become that this particular fly was one to eschew. Assuming that the fish had not been sufficiently frightened to leave its position, there was but one thing to do: rest it thoroughly, and while doing so, plan some method of attack which would put the fly—preferably a different size or pattern—within taking distance of the fish without any accompa-

nying ripples or waves to warn it of danger.

My friend agreed to the logic of this, but did not see any way of avoiding at least a few ripples when wading into the stream, unless he stood on our bank to cast— which was obviously out of the question, due not only to the distance, but also to lack of space for a back cast. I must confess that the outlook was not encouraging. The only chance I could see was to walk to the bottom of the pool, cross the stream in the fast water below it, and then quietly walk up the far bank to a group of rocks lying near the shore, forming a small peninsula out from the bank. With care it should be possible to wade out below these rocks without sending any ripples upstream along the bank to where the fish was supposed to be lying. Then a curve cast to the left might place the fly near enough the fish, with leader and line away from him, to induce a rise.

An awful lot of trouble, you say. So did my friend. But that is what had put the seven fish in my basket that morning, and is what will put them in yours on any heavily fished trout stream.

It was decided that I should be the goat, and I made my way across the stream, and got into position according to the plan, without sending any warning waves to the fish. Now, there was one thing in my favor which I had not noticed until I was ready to begin casting: At intervals a faint breeze wafted across the pool toward my bank where the fish lay—or was supposed to lie. Thought I to myself, if I put on a long, light leader, one of those little puffs will gently blow my fly as much as six feet, especially if I use a light, fluffy fly. Somewhat to the disgust of my expectant audience of one, I began changing my leader and fly. When I explained why, my friend settled back in a better humor.

At last—and it takes an awful long time to make a change at such a juncture—I was ready for the first all-important cast, with some twelve feet of leader, carrying at least five feet of 4X gut at the bottom, with a spider pattern up.

Next I made a high cast well short of the fish, to see just how the wind would act on the fly. The next puff carried it about four feet toward the bank, without any necessity for a curve cast, so I lengthened my line enough to reach the vital spot, and con-

tinued false casting until a puff of breeze started across the pool. It caught the fly in the air at the end of the forward cast and—gracefully blew it into the overhanging bushes.

"Haw! haw! haw!" from my friend. "All that trouble for nothing!"

I didn't feel so very happy, myself. But I remembered that the long hackles and the small hook on my spider fly provided a chance that it might not stick in the rhododendrons, and I carefully twitched the line a bit. It started to come, and the fly bounced from one rubberlike leaf to another until it finally drifted clear of them and fluttered to the water.

Simultaneously came a big swirl, and a yell from my friend. Just like any other human being I struck much too hard and left the spider with that trout, to say nothing of three links of beautiful 4X gut. And so it goes.

AUGUST 1936

ROBERT PAGE LINCOLN is remembered not for his trout fishing articles but for his fine books on bass and pike; his expertise extended to colder waters and species, though. In addition to writing articles, he served briefly as the fishing editor of *The Sportsman.* The tips he gives here are timeless.

TROUT FISHING IN FAST WATER

by ROBERT PAGE LINCOLN

O N WINTER evenings there is nothing more delightful to a fisherman, when he cannot exchange experiences with a fellow sportsman, than to pore over tales of trout lured out of their clear streams by a tiny midge-fly bait; of trout caught in vine-locked brooks where one must needs be a wizard not to break his rod in two; of the skill and the floaters which finally brought the dry-fly fisherman success. But after he has lighted his pipe for the tenth time and finished the story, he wonders why more has not been written of trout fishing in waters which crash and swirl and sweep everything—even unwary fishermen—before them; of the thrills of pulling big fellows out of midriver pools; and of all the tricks which have helped him to triumph. And as he puffs on, he draws pencil and paper toward him and writes.

And I shall write first—unconventionally, to be sure—about sharp-edged screws and hobnails, for when fishing swift waters you must first of all have a firm foothold. To grip and bite the slime-coated cobbles that too often pave the river beds nothing is equal to a series of sharp-edged screws turned in all over the soles of your shoes. Either half- or three-quarter-inch screws will do—according to the thickness of the soles—set an inch or a little less apart so that there may be room between to allow them to engage the rocks with which they come in contact. Hobnails wear down, and so become unsatisfactory; but you may trust yourself to sharp-edged screws, for they will keep their hold and save you many a spill.

Some there are who wear waist-high wading pants when going forth to do battle with trout in rushing waters. Under ordinary circumstances these are an advantage, but for this sort of fishing they are too bulky. When you find yourself being pulled into a frothing, foaming pool in a treacherous river you will find that you want to move more quickly and easily than ever before, and wading pants, besides filling and pulling you down, tend to keep you there. Even rubber boots under these conditions have proved the undoing of many a fisherman.

I wade such waters carefully and deliberately, a step at a time, wearing no boots, but simply a pair of heavy, thick-soled shoes set with screws to keep me in position. The water of most rivers is mild enough to be waded without chilling one through to the marrow, and a soaking does no harm. In the mountains, or wherever the water is of a lower temperature than usual, I have found it a protection to rub down briskly with melted tallow, lard, or vaseline, all parts of the body that stand a chance of being wet. Then I put on heavy woolen underwear and woolen socks and make trebly sure of my warmth by having another thorough rubdown on my return from fishing.

A river that is more or less swift must be studied carefully to be fished with anything approaching success. The choicest fish are not always found in the more easy-flowing water of a stream—they linger often in the eddied stretches avoided by the passing angler. Like most fishermen, I had walked miles upstream or downstream in search of calmer water before I decided that the trout I was looking for were in the stretch that I avoided, and made up my mind one day to break the charm of their retreat. I pushed forward and out, a step at a time, until I found a bar of sand and rock, by which I was able to reach nearly the middle of the river. And there I came upon the richest pool that I have ever fished. In it I caught brook trout, rainbow trout, brown trout, and no less than ten suckers—all on the lowly angleworm. The trout I was after were deep down, and one could as soon have had success fishing for them with bullfrogs as with flies along the surface. Indeed, I tried flies in every shape, size, coloration, time of day, and circumstance before I decided that angleworms were the only thing. And they were.

One of the rainbows caught in that pool of pools weighed a full six pounds, and I shall not forget that fight. The end of the bar where I stood was some distance from the river bank, and I must needs keep a taut line on the trout while making my way shoreward. I had already lost two fine trout before I cut myself a wading staff. With the staff in hand I was doubly sure of my footing—I waded shallow water with ease, and played every trout to advantage.

Remember the wading staff, O brother

Waltonians, should you elect to fish the swirling river. It may be cut in the rough, but to give it heft in the tip obtain a piece of iron pipe six inches long and two inches in diameter for a ferrule. Any blacksmith will weld to the end of this a tapering spike half an inch wide and six inches long. You can carry this ferrule along with you and fit it to your staff as you cut it in the wood. The pipe is held to the end of the staff by means of a nail or screw; but the iron should fit snugly, without wabbling. With this added heft, the staff is the more easily pushed through the water.

One of the best fishing places in the middle of a swift river is a spot where rocks or boulders rising above the surface ward off the onward torrent and form below them pools of more or less still water. Into these pools most of the trout within a wide radius will find their way, and there lie waiting for the river to toss down morsels from above. Especially before, during, or immediately after a rain will these pools provide good fishing possibilities. Trout seem to know instinctively that the rain will wash insects and all manner of earth creatures into the water. They are not too selective, and in the hurry to beat one another to the down-coming bait their ordinary caution is lost. I have caught trout one after another in these pools during a falling rain, leading each one out so as not to disturb the others.

Though the rainbow in my charmed pool was caught with a common "garden hackle," it must not be thought for a moment that angleworms are the only bait to bring the fisherman success in the rebellious reaches of a river. If that were so, much of the enchantment would be lost. The earthworm is necessary only where the pools are unusually deep. In those three feet deep or thereabout and well protected with boulders, the wet fly accounts for its share of the fine fellows. In such pools I have had extraordinary luck when I have used two flies on a leader and a baited hook. My system is to connect the back fly to the leader with a snell of gut eighteen inches long. I connect the middle fly, known as the dropper fly, to a snell twelve inches in length. Instead of a tip fly, I tie on a hook baited with an angleworm. Several split shot are nipped onto the leader above the baited hook to take it down. As it goes to the bottom, the flies on the longer-than-ordinary snells flash out downstream. An up-and-down movement of the rod at this point makes the line active and also causes the flies to move. The fact that there are usually a number of trout in a midriver pool makes competition keen, and often both flies and worm are set upon. It is no fish story to report having caught two trout at once by following this procedure.

In small, clear streams where everything that falls on the surface betrays itself as genuine or a fraud, there is no wonder that the smaller trout flies are in demand; in some cases the very smallest ones, especially dry flies, are properly in their element. Where the water is constantly fretted and obscured by currents, cross eddies, and the myriad disturbing things identified with swift water, the trout have not the same chance to study what comes along. When food appears, it is seized. I believe that the number 8 fly is the best all-round size for wild waters. When I am fishing rainbow trout I use number 4 and number 6 during the day, and larger flies toward dusk. In that maelstrom of liquid fury, St. Mary's Rapids, the number 1 bass flies during the twilight are the best of all; indeed, I would use nothing smaller at that hour.

Some anglers use shotted flies which are prepared by nipping a heavy shot onto the hook of the fly itself, while others make flies with lead inner bodies just heavy enough to resist the water and not be carried along too fast. Weighted flies are to be bought, but they are all alarmingly large. A little study of the fish you want and its environment will enable you to determine the right weight of bait to use for wild-water trout fishing.

To offset the disadvantages in swift-river fishing, such as difficulty in reaching the midriver pools, there are certain advantages. The sound of your approach is covered, to a degree, at least, by the noise of rushing water. In spite of the grating of the shod wading staff, you can often come within four or five yards of a deep pool and catch the fish at your feet. It is true that the water, being swift, has a tendency to seize the bait or flies and carry them away from the trout too speedily, while, if the leader is weighed down with too much shot, it is hard to tell when to set the hook. This is a matter, however, to be judged by practice and a particular study of casting in fast water.

When the shore falls off so steeply that wading out is impossible, I use a boat to reach the alluring midstream pools. First I attach a wire from a tree on one shore to another tree directly across the stream. Then I let down the boat by means of a clothesline rope fastened to an iron ring that slides along the wire. By moving the ring forward on the wire and allowing plenty of line, it is easy to reach exactly the position from which I wish to cast into the pool. One can fish the wildest water in this manner—indeed, one can have wires at intervals here and there over the best pools and drop downstream from one to another. After fishing a pool, it is a simple matter to pull the boat by means of the rope back to the wire and thence back to shore. The only essential requirement of the cross-stream wire is that it be strong and securely held in place.

The average fisherman not acquainted

with the habits of the trout cannot imagine finding them in swift waters. Yet right off the foam at the foot of crashing falls I have caught them. Strange, indeed, are these trout; but they love the swift water. And the man who would have the most sport trout fishing will seek them in their wild recesses. Then he, too, will gloat over successes that have come from a knowledge of their ways, and on winter nights he will recall past victories, and dream, as his pipe draws well, of turbulent waters, hungry trout, dusky twilight, drizzly days, and future conquests.

JULY 1927

MAKING THE MOST OF TROUT WATERS

OBSERVE YOUR STREAM AND ITS POSSIBILITIES
IF YOU WOULD FISH YOUR FLY OVER FISH

by EUGENE V. CONNETT III

I CONFESS THAT when I had succeeded in composing that rather hopeful title, such things as stocking and physical improvement of the stream were dancing before my eyes. Having composed it, I realized—pen in hand—what a devilish job that meant, and, being exceedingly lazy, I decided to get out from under. We shall therefore, dear readers, gently shove off in another direction.

It should be entirely evident that more important results may be expected when one is fishing the fly over a fish than when one is not. It would, indeed, be illuminating to have an actual record of the percentage of casts made over a trout as against those made over empty water. If such an invaluable set of statistics could be obtained, I venture to say that less time would be spent in pushing a fly rod and more in observing the stream and its possibilities.

It is very easy to waste precious hours on an unfamiliar stream. For instance, in water where one has definitely located fish lying under the banks in April, hours may be consumed in trying to raise these fish in mid-May. They have moved into new positions with the falling water. Ensues a period of searching the stream at large for them, and not until their whereabouts are discovered can any serious attempts to catch them be undertaken. Early in June the May flies come on, and rising fish advertise their positions clearly. With the necessity for seeking them goes the necessity for small baskets. We are apt, by the way, to give full credit for a good basket in May-fly time to the avidity with which the trout feed. We must also give weight to the fact that it is no longer necessary to locate them, and that we are thus able to spend the greater part of our time in productive fishing over trout which indicate their positions by continual rises.

Knowing that the fish lay under the banks in our particular water this April, and remembering what sort of places they took up in May when the stream had run down, we shall be able next spring to save a great deal of nonproductive time in searching for them. Fortunately for the fish and our sport, the stream will have been materially changed by autumn and spring floods, and we shall still have to exercise a dash of intelligence in putting our fingers on fish. We shall find this boulder and that holding a trout as usual, but we shall also discover that this deep run is now choked with rubble, while that flat shallow has been scooped out to form a splendid hiding place. So I shall give you an extraordinarily good bit of advice—which, of course, you won't act on: Put in most of your day exploring the stream, familiarizing yourself with the new state of the bottom, discovering what that swirl means, and what this slick hides. Then you are all set to kill a few

fish tomorrow, or at least to spend most of your time fishing over trout instead of stones.

Having—I hope—established the fact that large baskets are in great part due to the productive use of time on the stream, which in turn can be largely achieved through an intimate knowledge of the water, may I go on to point out that large baskets are not necessarily either your ambition or mine. Once we are content in the knowledge that we can fill such a basket, with conditions reasonably favorable, we are most likely to be content to let the other fellow spend his time doing it. Our inclinations will probably lead us to seek the very large fish, or perhaps the most difficult fish, regardless of their size.

I have watched the paths of a number of my experienced angling friends as they traveled out of the lower realms of fly-fishing, and it is beyond peradventure that those to whom the big fish most appeal have curiously grown less and less "purist," in that they find pleasure in the use of bucktails, spinners, and such lures for the monsters of the stream. Something in the neighborhood of sixteen inches becomes their lower limit of ambition. They are very valuable anglers, as their efforts keep the dangerous cannibals down to a reasonable limit; but they are cheating themselves of a tremendous amount of pleasure. We simple-minded fellows, who are content to "waste" an hour over a ten- or twelve-inch fish in a position which makes him as difficult to catch as you like, and who find our satisfaction in playing the game according to some self-imposed set of rules or restrictions, are really getting more fun out of the sport. We can fish with pleasure in a stream where a trout a foot long is the maximum; we can enjoy a day immensely whether our basket is heavy or light. And I am sure that we suffer the loss of a big one with far less acute pain. I, for one, believe that mental anguish and fly-fishing do not belong together; I can find plenty of the former without seeking it on a trout stream.

Consider for a moment the relative values involved in my struggle to take a difficultly placed ten-inch fish, and that of my friend seeking the eighteen-inch trout of his dreams. I am just as intently engrossed in my efforts as he is; I am exhibiting just as much skill—let us whisper it!—if not more, than he is; my pleasure is just as keen if I succeed as is his if he succeeds; but my sorrow, if I fail, is assuaged by the knowledge that I can find another difficult fish a few hundred yards upstream. Can my friend? Once or twice a month—in a rising mood. I can return at night happy, while he must rest under a shadow of sorrow and regret until he can locate another big one on the feed.

Now, mind you, I *have* lost some fearfully big trout, and have even carried the thought of them home with me; but they haven't spoiled my outlook on life—in fact, one of my good fishing friends has more than once become quite annoyed with my lack of appreciation for the proper wailing and gnashing of teeth upon the occasions of losing several really big fish. As a corollary, he has been even more annoyed at my lack of the proper enthusiasm upon having landed several equally big fish. And to add to these unnatural misconceptions of mine, I have even bored him with quite unreasonable enthusiasm in connection with the difficulty of catching some trout which certainly did not measure more than a dozen inches in length. Having honestly and fearlessly acknowledged my failings, may I say that his too great appreciation of the necessity for bemoaning the loss of a big fish gives me a sharp, shooting pain? On the other hand, I can easily join him in his joy at the capture of a big one.

There is one very practical consideration in connection with this matter of being able to find contentment and pleasure in the minor problems of the stream as against the necessity of taking big fish in order to get a kick out of fly-fishing. On all of the streams within easy striking distance of our large centers of population, our fishing range is decidedly restricted—either through the multitude of anglers found on open waters or because of the naturally restricted range of any member on club waters.

Even the open waters in remote districts are becoming crowded because of good automobile roads and the increasing use of airplanes by sportsmen. Restricted range is a serious matter to the angler who is only interested in big fish; but the fly-fisherman who enjoys the problems offered by difficult fish—more or less regardless of their avoirdupois—need not view with undue alarm his fellow man, if the latter has the instincts of a gentleman. In other words, in order to make the most of restricted water, seek pleasure in the niceties of the sport rather than in the weight of the quarry.

And now for a plunge in a rather unhappy direction. Instead of entering this particular bit of very cold water inch by inch, I will flop right down in it. Open fishing in and near thickly populated sections is soon either going to be a thing of the past or at least a thing holding little pleasure for the fly-fisherman. It is true that such streams may be teeming with stocked trout, but it is equally true that for each trout there is a fisherman—to put it mildly. I defy anyone to thread his way through these hordes of patient worm enthusiasts trying to cast a fly. They are patient, by the way, because they have to stand in one place in order not to get their legs tangled in all the lines around them. If any reader thinks I am exaggerating, let him visit the Musconetcong River in New Jersey on the opening day of the trout season; I dare say it is no worse than others within fifty miles of a large city.

As there is no particularly good reason why a fly-fisherman should have to travel hundreds of miles in order to enjoy his sport, he naturally is renting fishing rights somewhat nearer home, and every time he does this—which is often—he helps to make my prediction come nearer being a *fait accompli*. It may be news to many that such rivers as the Rogue in Oregon are rapidly being bought up by anglers, and it is to be expected that many good streams nearer the large cities will be closed to the public. In other words, trout fishing rights are rapidly assuming concrete values, as is the case in England. Theoretically, this is a shame; practically, it is a necessity, and we may as well start to accustom ourselves to the thought. In the case of shooting, the thing will soon be done; there are whole counties without an acre of open shooting today. Based upon a thoroughly practical and first-hand experience with this matter, I can say that properly handled private trout waters afford more sport than do public. By the time my son is as old and gray as I am, the only good fly-fishing will be in private waters. In giving this warning I almost drop my fly on the title of this article.

APRIL 1930

EUGENE V. CONNETT III

142

DRY-FLY FISHING—NOW AND THEN

A LIGHT ROD IS ESSENTIAL FOR THE FOLLOWER

OF THE AMERICAN METHOD

by SAMUEL G. CAMP

IN A SMALL advertising folder which I was reading not long ago a new model of what many believe to be the world's best fly rod was briefly described as follows: "New pattern specially desirable Dry Fly Rod, powerful but not too stiff; beautiful sweet action and design; eight feet in length, and four ounces weight."

Now, perhaps that doesn't mean so much to the recent dry-fly recruit who has been well advised in the selection of his tackle, but to some of us who have been in the game since the dry fly had its coming-out party in this country it means a lot. To me those few words very closely represent the consensus of opinion of expert dry-fly anglers all over the country, after an experimental period of some twenty years,

as to the sort of dry-fly rod, all things considered, best adapted to the general run of American trout waters under the conditions usually encountered—and what a different sort of rod it is from the ones which years ago we were led to believe were imperative for best results in casting and in fishing the floater!

The first book on dry-fly fishing to appear in this country was Emlyn M. Gill's *Practical Dry-Fly Fishing*, published in 1912. It was a notably well-written work as well as a very persuasive brief for the use of the dry fly on American streams, and to it may safely be attributed the beginning of the present popularity of the surface feathers on American waters. Prior to the appearance of Mr. Gill's work, dry-fly fishing was little practiced and less written about over here. The few American anglers who did, to a greater or lesser extent, experiment with the floater, were readers and followers of England's famous exponent of the dry fly, Frederic M. Halford. In all, Mr. Halford was the author of seven books. The first, *Floating Flies and How to Dress Them,* was published in 1886; the last, *The Dry-Fly Man's Handbook,* appeared in 1913. He was the acknowledged court of last resort in all matters pertaining to the dry fly—and inferentially, at least, he had little use for what, even from the American viewpoint at the time, might by any manner of means be considered light tackle. George La Branche and his book, *The Dry Fly in Fast Water,* were also influential in the development of dry-fly fishing in America.

Naturally enough, our pioneer dry-fly anglers were afflicted with what might be termed a heavy-tackle complex. To be sure, Mr. Gill paid his respects in no uncertain terms to the "weapons" suggested by some English angling writers, advising for use on American streams rods from nine to ten feet in length. But, doubtless in deference to the Halford tradition, he described the ten-foot rod as being "perhaps the favorite"— the average split-bamboo fly rod in this length weighing six ounces or more. Other writers followed suit. There was a fixed belief that at least a moderately heavy and proportionately powerful rod was necessary

for dry-fly fishing. As an example of what I mean, I might cite the case of a deservedly popular angling book published in 1919, in which the author advises a rod of "not less than nine and one-half feet, and with considerable backbone" as necessary for dry-fly fishing—and I am by no means passing up a certain small volume for which I was personally responsible, and which is open to criticism in the same respect.

It is a matter for regret that back in the dark ages of the dry fly in America we did not pay more heed to the words of that able and thoroughly self-reliant English angling writer, Mr. G.E.M. Skues, who, in his book, *Minor Tactics of the Chalk Stream,* published in 1910, or some two years prior to Mr. Gill's pioneer American work on the dry fly, came out very strongly for the use of light tackle on British dry-fly waters.

To put it in brief, in *Minor Tactics* Mr. Skues tells the story of how he happened to be "down on the Itchen" the afternoon on which a two-and-one-eighth-pound trout was killed on a very light rod of a famous American make, the rod belonging to one of two American anglers who were fishing the stream on that occasion. One of the American anglers, Mr. Skues continues, "was fishing with a nine-foot rod weighing five ounces, a delightful tool capable of casting a heavy tapered Halford line with wonderful command. I had the privilege of trying it, and I promptly acquired its duplicate, in addition to the ten-footer of the same make which I already possessed and had used the previous season." And in a footnote, in the third edition of *Minor Tactics*, 1924, Mr. Skues says that this rod, after eighteen years' hard wear, is still his favorite. Now, had more of us, over here, started with the proposition that a nine-foot, five-ounce rod was fully up to the very exacting requirements of the British dry-fly waters—but that is water under the bridge, after all these years. At any rate, following

America's discovery of the dry fly, came a period of use and experiment during which it has become increasingly apparent that, as regards the rods best suited to the game as we play it, the shorter and lighter rods have it all over the longer and heavier articles. In discussing fly rods it is probably necessary to say that I am speaking in terms of split-bamboo. In fact, as the situation is described by one of our best-known rod-making concerns, "It is now only a question of how short and how light a rod can be used and give perfect satisfaction to the dry-fly angler."

This conclusion has been reached through a gradual awakening to the fact that it is quite a long walk, as well as a lengthy swim, from the Beaverkill, let us say, to the Itchen or the Test—that American and English dry-fly fishing are two quite different propositions. It is more a matter of methods than of stream conditions, though, of course, stream conditions give rise to methods. The English dry-fly purist casts only to rising trout, and, consequently, with more or less frequent periods of rest. The American dry-fly artist fishes all the water, casting continually—and if you know the real fly-fishing fanatic, you'll know I mean he casts *continually*. And there you are. The British dry-fly man, if he so chooses, can use quite a hefty

fly rod without cracking under the strain. But when, to the casts required in the process of getting the line out, you add the innumerable false casts necessary for keeping the fly in a floating condition—a fly, remember, which is on the water most of the time—it should not be difficult to realize that, for comfort in long continued casting, a light rod is essential for the follower of the American dry-fly method.

For general stream fishing, wherever light tackle can be employed with reasonable safety, eight-foot dry-fly rods, weighing four ounces or a fraction under, are endorsed by the leading experts. On the smaller streams, rods of seven to seven and a half feet are not uncommon. And such dry-fly rods—the reference is to the higher-grade articles turned out by our best makers—will be found in material and action fully up to the work at hand. For the sake of brevity I have steered clear of the matter of rod action, but I might just repeat for emphasis that the present tendency is away from the excessively stiff models. The dry-fly beginner, who, perhaps, has been reading up on the subject in some of the older angling books, might with some advantage to himself think over the above suggestions regarding the matter of rod selection.

The radical change of view, with regard to the right sort of rod for fishing with a dry fly, would seem to be the most important development since the introduction of the surface feathers over here. But of little less significance is the modern view as regards the dry fly itself—that is, as to the type of fly best suited to American streams. Years ago we used to hear a good deal about "exact imitation"—matching the artificial fly with the natural. Because we had no artificial replicas of the natural insects common to our trout streams, it was generally conceded that we were working under a very considerable handicap. Little, however, has been done to alter the situation, perhaps because of the very practical fact that small flies of the exact imitation type, when used for fishing all the water, and on the fast water so common to our trout streams, are difficult to keep in a floating condition, and, likewise, hard to see. To be thoroughly adapted to the American dry-fly method, the fly should be easy to float and easy to see.

Thus we have come to the very general use of the Bivisible Hackle dry flies, the merits of which were so convincingly brought out by Mr. E.R. Hewitt in his book, *Telling on the Trout,* and also the very popular fanwing series of floaters. The bivisible hackles, whether the Brown Bivisible, the Gray Bivisible, or whatever the pattern, have a wisp of white hackle wound at the head of the fly, thus putting the fly, when on the water, in something of the same class as the celebrated Coachman in the matter of visibility. Having no wings, of course, the Bivisible Hackle dry fly does not have to be "cocked," and, for the same reason, is much more durable than the conventional winged variety of fly. Likewise, the Bivisible Hackles ride "high and dry" on the surface, and are very easy to keep that way.

MAY 1931

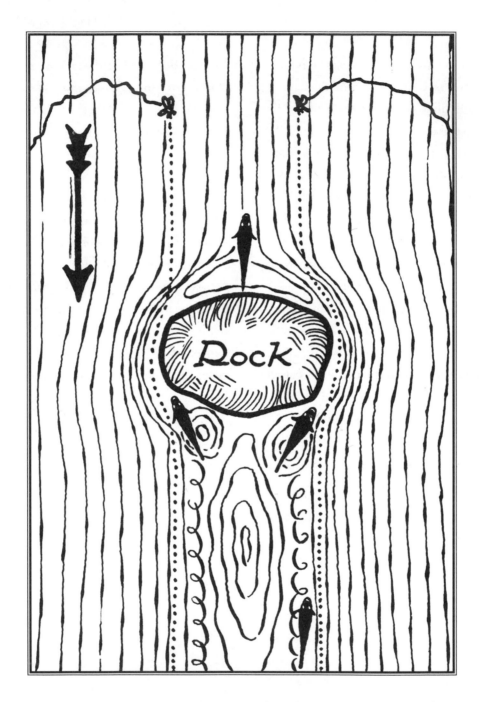

FIG. 1. *An approximate map of the situation about the rock from which four fish were raised. It was on casts made from three to six feet above the rock that every fish was taken.*

ANGLING CLOSE-UPS

HOW TO RAISE FOUR FISH AROUND A ROCK
WHERE ONE WAS THOUGHT TO LIE

by EUGENE V. CONNETT III

MANY TROUT fishermen never bother with the details of catching fish, but rely rather on a sort of bird's-eye view of the water and a somewhat general method of covering it. They catch trout, but miss half the fun of the game— and a great many fish as well— by not interesting themselves in the niceties involved in taking individual and often difficult fish.

I recall several situations of which I made a rather careful study, during the course of which I learned a lot about trout. One of them involved a certain isolated rock in the "Big" Beaverkill, past which the water flowed fairly fast and was somewhere between my knees and my waist in depth. If I had not been exceedingly curious and

perhaps ridiculously patient, I should have been content to raise one fish around this rock, and gone on my way rejoicing. As it was, I raised four, and instead of passing on to further triumphs spent an hour or so studying the rock, the currents around it, and the behavior of live flies passing it, as well as the necessities involved in making my fly act as they did.

In the diagram (fig. 1) is shown an approximate map of the situation. The upstream side of the rock shelved down into the water for several inches and then dropped suddenly to the stream bed. Under each side of the rock the bottom had been slightly cut away. Downstream from the rock was a sandy-bottomed backwater. The day before I had seen a fish slide up on to the shelving upstream surface of the rock to take a fly, and slip gently back into the depths. This day I saw a fish rise on the right-hand side of the rock. Being in no hurry and in an optimistic frame of mind, I approached the rock trying to convince myself that instead of having seen one fish rise in two places, I had seen two different fish come up.

In order to float my fly past the side of the rock without drag, I had to take up a position below and to the right. Then a loose curve cast which placed the fly above the rock permitted it to float down to it and on past it without drag. When the fly had passed the rock, and reached a point several feet below it, still traveling in the current without drag, what should happen but a fish take it! This fellow had been lying on the edge of the current, in the still backwater below the rock, but I did not know this until later. At any rate, I landed him without messing up the water around the rock, and then began floating my fly down past the right-hand side of it once more. On about the tenth cast up popped a fish from beside the rock, took the fly, dashed down under the rock, and sawed off my leader against it. Fish number two. Whether he left the vicinity or just lay doggo under his end of the rock, I am not certain.

By this time I was all set for further miracles, and began to operate on the the-

ory that there was a fish lying in the cushion of still water where the current hit the upstream side of the rock. At least, I had seen one rise there the day before. An exaggerated curve cast, with plenty of slack line, and the fly came down head on for the middle of the upstream side of the rock. This is about as difficult a cast as there is, because the battle isn't over until the fly has surged up to the rock, backed away a little, and then swung on around the rock in the fast current. Without plenty of slack, there will be a drag before this performance has been completed.

I made the grade four times without an error, when a fish rose just in front of the rock, took the fly, and broke my leader. At least, I like to think he broke it, although I was a bit excited by his appearance and may have struck like a fool. However, he was fish number three.

Not a little ashamed of myself, but still possessed of a wild desire to see what was under the other end of that rock, I worked around into a new position, below and to the left of it, so that I could float a fly down past the only virgin water left. To put it very mildly, I'm damned if I didn't raise another fish here, only to have him saw off my leader as his partner on the right-hand side of that same ragged rock had done.

While I admit that every rock in the Beaverkill doesn't hold four fish, I do aver that a great many anglers will not take the trouble to prove it. Most of them decide that there is one fish in one position around the rock—either from having seen him rise there, or because experience indicates the most likely looking spot; or else they put a fly past one side or the other of the rock where the danger of drag is least. If they take one fish from the vicinity, most of them will move on to the next rock, entirely satisfied.

Now, in taking the fish around this rock, I discovered that a fly placed right beside it did no execution. It was on casts made from three to six feet above the rock that every fish was taken. Whether this was due to the fact that the fish had been educated to distrust flies dropped on the water close to the rock—the way the average angler would be likely to drop them in order to avoid the necessity of overcoming a very difficult problem in drag—or whether they could not see the fly unless it was coming down to them from above, due to their being in the scooped-out hole under the edge of the rock, I am not prepared to say. Experience with a number of other rocks has convinced me, however, that it pays to learn how to float a fly down from above, around the edge, and well below without drag. The problems involved can most easily be learned by standing back of such a rock and studying the water in great detail,

until one has a perfect picture of its behavior. Then practice casting around the rock until a fly can be floated past, free of drag. It sounds easy but isn't.

———

In a good trout stream where the fish are fairly plentiful it certainly pays to assume that there is more than one fish around a favorably placed rock of any size. If there should be but one, it pays to fish as though there were several, for there is no way of telling in which position the one may be, unless he is seen to rise.

Fig. 2 shows an actual arrangement of rocks along the bank, and one which is quite common to a number of streams. This place is also on the "Big" Beaverkill. Starting at the upstream end of the picture, we find three small rocks against the bank, one below the other. In each indentation between them is a quiet little eddy, the edge of the main current of the stream being slowed up where it borders the rocks. As the current strikes the upstream face of the big boulder, it is compressed and increases in speed. At the lower corner of the boulder it passes on straight downstream, forming a small eddy, below which is a large one. Along the edge of the current, below the boulder, is a quiet lane of water. I have indicated the positions of nine fish, and as I have at various times taken fish from each

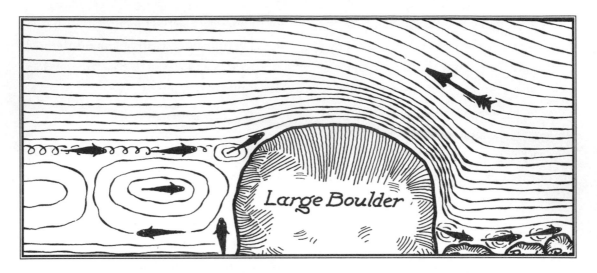

FIG. 2. *An arrangement of rocks along the bank quite common to a number of streams. The positions of nine fish are indicated, from each of which positions fish have at various times been taken.*

of these positions, it is safe to assume that they either hold nine different trout or are occupied by one or more fish at different times.

The upper three present no great difficulties in the way of drag, except that the line must be kept out of the faster current around the boulder. The three lying along the edge of the current below the boulder look easier than they are. The fly should be dropped near the upstream edge of the boulder and floated past it, as close to the edge of the current as possible. If it gets on to the slower water, it will drag at once; if it is not near the slower water, it is doubtful if the fish will come out to it, unless they are decidedly on the feed.

When we come to the fish lying in the whirlpool and quiet water beyond it, our troubles begin. The only way in which I know how to put a fly over these fish is by casting many feet up in the air above them, allowing the leader to fall in loose coils on the surface. As the line is caught by the current, the leader uncoils, allowing the fly to rest on the water for some seconds before it is dragged away. The sad part of this story is that the fly must not be permitted to be dragged away, but must be picked up cleanly before this happens. Unless the fish is feeding, it is almost impossible to bring him up by repeated casting, because an error is practically unavoidable in the course of a dozen such casts.

A thing that deserves careful study is the way that fast water flows past slow water—in other words, the edges of currents. There seems to be a cushion between the two that is particularly suited to trout. I used to think that they lay in the still water, and came out of it into the current to take flies. Some undoubtedly do just that, but many others lie in the very streak where the fast water rubs along against the slow. I have actually seen them there when they were on the feed and therefore close to the surface. There are two possible explanations for this: The surface of this streak may be peculiarly suited to collecting flies as they float downstream; or there may be some mechanical peculiarity in the streak which renders it a pleasant place for a trout to lie. Perhaps both explanations apply. At any rate, it requires some study to float a fly properly on the very edge of this streak, for if the fly is too far from it, trout often will not take it, while if it is directly on the streak drag soon develops. To me this fishing is one of the niceties of angling.

The streak need not be just below a rock; it may be in comparatively open water. Nor must it be a very obvious streak; it may be one that can only be discovered by close observation of the surface. In any event it will prove well worth a lot of attention on the trout fisherman's part.

I have proved to my entire satisfaction that on comparatively smooth water which is not moving too fast, much better results are obtained by floating a fly from a point well above the fish down over him, than by dropping it on his nose. When a fish is found feeding just under a branch that closely overhangs the water, it is a temptation to drop the fly as close to the downstream side of the foliage as possible. Fish do take such a fly; but I am confident that for every time they do, they would take it five times if it had come down to them from above the branch. Here is fine opportunity for finesse. In most cases the cast must be made from a point almost across from the branch, instead of from below. One must remember to keep out of the trout's range of vision—perhaps by bending close to the water and using a low side cast. Very often an exaggerated curve must be given the line and leader, and a Scotchman had better leave the matter severely alone, as the fly must be allowed to float right into the twigs in many instances. By pulling it out smoothly and carefully it can usually be retrieved without loss, while in an astonishing number of cases it will float right on through a most awful-looking tangle, and emerge safely below the branch. The latter procedure is, of course, the thing to strive for, as pulling the fly across the water to you will probably annoy the fish.

Just as it is worth while to float a fly down from several feet above the fish, so does it pay to let the fly float on past him for some distance. Don't wait until a drag sets up, however. Many a trout keeps his eye on your fly long after it has passed below him—especially if there is no real hatch on—and seeing it continue quietly and naturally on its way must help to convince him that it is a safe morsel. You never know when he is drifting down under it, and you never know when he will turn and rush for it. These extended floats call for great precautions against drag, and one should study the difficulties to be over-come before making the cast. Should the fly drag on the first cast, it is well to put on a new fly, or change the size, before making the second cast. An impatient angler will not trouble with such details, but will either waste his time over a nervous fish or go on to the next. More power to his elbow, but he misses a lot of fun.

About the finest fishing we have in this country is to be found in a bouldery stream holding good brown trout. This is "pocket" fishing—working over trout that lie in ei-ther large or small pockets between the boulders, which are often submerged. The position of a pocket can be discovered by a study of the surface. One will notice a slick amongst the twisting surface currents, and with practice recognize the presence of a pocket—not directly under the slick in all cases, but often above it. The fly should be a good floater, such as a "Shaving-Brush" Hackle, and should be dropped on the water with a short line. Visibility is low in broken water, and it is usually safe to get quite close to the trout. A float of twelve inches may be as much as you can achieve on a small slick, but that is often enough. Sometimes one merely whisks the fly to the surface for an instant, and picks it up again. This is about all that can be done when it must be dropped above the slick in rough water. These pocket trout waste no time in rising; if they don't come up quick their din-ner is gone. Long floats are therefore unnec-essary. Don't imagine that a small pocket means a small fish; someday you will have heart failure if you do. And don't think that it doesn't pay to fish pocket water thor-oughly. It is hard work to make these quick, short casts, on the *qui vive* for a slashing rise at any instant, but the results are excit-ing and productive.

JUNE 1930

⟪ EUGENE V. CONNETT III ⟫

154

GEORGE D.B. BONBRIGHT was ahead of his time. While A.W. Dimock wrote about the possibilities of tarpon on the fly in 1911, few heeded his words, and most continued to toss hardware and plugs at these splendid game fish. This article was the real beginning of a new sport.

TAKING TARPON WITH A FLY

HERE'S THE WHERE AND HOW OF IT IF
TARPON FISHING YOU WOULD GO

by GEORGE D.B. BONBRIGHT

FLY-FISHING for tarpon is not a new idea. It has been known for many years that, under certain conditions, tarpon, especially the smaller ones, can be taken in this way. I can remember reading several interesting articles telling of the great sport to be had in Panama fishing for small tarpon, and Mr. Dimock in his book, *The Book of the Tarpon,* tells thrilling tales of big and little fish taken on the fly.

Being an ardent fly-fisherman for salmon and trout, I was tremendously interested in everything I could learn on this subject; but, as a matter of fact, I could find very little definite information from sources I had available. However, on numerous fishing trips taken in Florida during the last few years, I have gathered considerable data pertaining to the details and tackle best suited for the taking of these wonderful fish on the fly, and I am tempted to set these down in the hope that fellow fishermen and friends may, perhaps, more easily find success, and enjoy the great thrill and sport which has come to me in my last two trips to the east coast of Florida.

First of all, as to the fish itself: A tarpon has always thrilled me, even from my first attempts at still-fishing on the west coast over thirty years ago. To me, there is something about the wild, unbridled leap of the tarpon when first hooked that, as a sporting experience, puts it in a class by itself. Many a day I have started out to fish for sailfish, or perhaps planned a day for bonefish, but the chance sight of a rolling tarpon has changed it all for me and, if I had any choice in the matter, tarpon fishing I would go.

I first hooked a tarpon on a fly on one of the upper reaches of St. Lucie River. There was one spot there called Tarpon Pool where a few fish seemed to stay all through the winter months. I just lived with those fish, trying every bait I ever heard of to get one to bite, but without success, until one day I took out a heavy trout rod, and with a large fly began casting for snook, a number of which I had seen break water near-by. I got no snook, but I did have a fifty-pound tarpon do his best to get the fly. He startled me so that I pulled it away, and he would not come again. However, I did hook two tarpon that season up around Tarpon Pool. One bit the heavy gut leader in two, and the second disappeared in the depths just as we were attempting to gaff him, the leader having pulled off the end of the casting line. I made up my mind then and there to go after tarpon in earnest with a fly at the first opportunity, and began planning flies and tackle that I thought might prove suitable for the work.

My most recent trip was in the latter part of May of this year. We were met at Long Key by Capt. Walter Starck and his comfortable cruising house boat, *Norma II,* and we enjoyed a wonderful ten days. Our party of four, using live bait and artificial shrimp, landed sixty big tarpon, the average

weight probably being close to one hundred pounds, and the largest tipping the scales at one hundred and sixty pounds. In addition, I landed sixty-two fish, all on a fly, the average weight of these being about twenty pounds. The big fish usually stay in the large, deeper passes, and for that reason are not so easily taken on a fly. They will come after it if they can see it, but they are hard to get to the surface. Except for a few fish, kept for mounting and photographing, all were released to live and bite another day.

The best places in Florida to catch tarpon on a fly are the smaller passes both above and below Long Key. The fish hang quite close to the openings in the trestle of the Florida East Coast Railway, each opening forming a pool in itself and holding generally from one to a dozen fish that have taken their position to feed on the luckless small fry coming through with the tide. With clear water and a bright day, one can see these fish. It is an interesting fact that tarpon are easily frightened, and it is not often that one can hook more than one or two from a single arch. A jumping fish seems to act as a warning to the others that all is not well, and they will not bite again until rested. In this connection, we have found that, even in somewhat larger passes, we seldom get good tarpon fishing two days in succession. The only exception to this appears to be in the Bahía Honda, where the taking of any number of fish seems to make no difference in their biting on the next tide. Of course, the Bahía Honda is an extremely wide, deep pass, and there are times when, on windy days, it gets much too rough for canoe fishing. Fishing must then be done from launches, although this method is not as satisfactory.

The equipment for fly-fishing must be carefully chosen if one is to have any success at all. A few trout may be taken on almost any kind of tackle, but this cannot be done with tarpon. First of all, one should have a short, stiff rod, nine feet to nine feet, three inches, weight ten to eleven ounces, preferably with two joints, although three will answer the purpose. The rod should have a small handle below the reel seat. One might land a twenty-pound tarpon on a four-ounce trout rod, but the rod would not stand many encores; and if you should happen, as I did this last spring, to hook an occasional eighty-five-pounder, you would find the eleven-ounce rod quite small enough. The first of these big fish was on for about fifteen minutes, jumped seven times, and finally threw the hook out. This fish went where he pleased, and we had very little control over him. The second, hooked in a small pass and in fairly shallow water, seemed exhausted after fifteen minutes of wild running and jumping. We had worked our canoe close to the shore, and my boatman had jumped overboard to take

hold of the wire leader with the idea of beaching him when the hook tore out and the fish slowly swam away. We could have gaffed this last fish, if we had wished to. A salmon rod, or a long rod of any kind, is not good in a canoe; it is hard to handle and you cannot get near your fish or get hold of your leader. For a reel, we use Edward Vom Hofe Tobique 2/o with forty yards of heavy level, size D, waterproof line, and lots of backing. The leader should be of fine wire with a very small swivel on the end of the wire to which to attach the line.

The fly is the most important item of the equipment. There may be, and is, a great difference of opinion as to why a salmon takes a fly, but there can be no doubt that a tarpon takes it because he thinks it is something good to eat. Inasmuch as he feeds largely on shrimp and minnows, it is necessary to approach in appearance one or both of these as near as possible. For the same reason, any fly for tarpon should be fished rather deep with a shrimplike movement, and not drawn on the surface. The fly that I have named Tarpon White seems to meet all requirements and, I think, will raise fish if anything will. This fly is the result of much experimenting and many changes. It is a wonderfully showy fly in the water, with silver body and flexible white wings, a strip of golden pheasant crest on each side to add glint and reflect light, then a red feather for the gills and jungle cock for the eye, and, last of all, a touch of red in the tail to suggest blood on a wounded minnow.

The Lady Amherst, a fly which has proved a great success for salmon on the Grand Cascapedia River, has also been found very successful with tarpon. These patterns were tied for me by Messrs. Forest & Sons of Kelsoe, Scotland, and are tied on a long-shanked hook 21 $1/16$ and 3$1/4$ inches in length, with a 5/0 bend of hook. This gives a long, showy fly with the advantage of reasonably small wire that penetrates easily. The ordinary hook of this length would be an 8/0 or a 9/0.

In playing the fish, it will be found advisable to wear a glove on the left hand, so that you can hold the line without its cutting your fingers as it slips through. Even the heavy brake on these reels is, at times, not sufficient pressure to stop a tarpon. Other fish take the fly as well as tarpon and there will be times when it will be necessary to hold the line and let something break. A case of this kind happened to me this spring. I had just hooked a snapper about four pounds in weight, when there was a tremendous swirl in the water and the fin of a large shark appeared. There was not much argument as to who got the snapper, for that shark weighed five hundred pounds, if he weighed an ounce. He must have been surprised at the strength of the snapper when it took a forty-pound pull on my part to break him loose.

It is an interesting fact that tarpon will leap to almost unbelievable heights. The opening in the trestle is fully fifteen feet high, and there are times when the fish seem to go up level with the top of these openings.

Although when fishing with a fly the number of tarpon landed compared to the number of strikes is small, to me the thrill of seeing the silver kings take the fly and the realization that the fight is a more evenly balanced one more than compensates for the weight of the larger fish, and I heartily recommend this type of fishing to any fellow sportsman.

SEPTEMBER 1929

OLD-TIMER

OF THIS FINE FISHING STORY ONE CAN ONLY SAY
THAT IT IS IN THE TRUE TRADITION OF THE FOLLOWERS
OF WALTON AND COTTON

by HOWARD T. WALDEN II

MILL AND I had finished our sandwiches and sat smoking our pipes in the calm of the high noon. An angler was coming into sight around the far bend downstream. At two hundred yards it is not easy to distinguish features and form, yet we were able to see at once that this noonday adventurer was neither kid nor novice. He was full of years and full of experience. Thigh-deep, he poled himself along in midcurrent with a five-foot staff, braced himself against it, and cast across and upstream. Here was a thorough-going angler with a simple and effective system. He would fish every yard of water fifty or sixty feet above him, retrieve, plug ahead with the staff to within ten feet of the previous casts' limits, and repeat the rou-

tine of throwing flies. There was a slow inevitability about him; he drew nearer to us as the hand of a watch draws nearer the hour. For some minutes we regarded him intently, without speaking; and as he wore along, upstream, it became increasingly manifest that we were watching a supreme stylist. A grace as ancient and inbred as that of the oak under which we sat was implicit in that casting. The rhythm never varied; the man and the rod were as one, as if the rod were a physical extension of the man. The back cast was exquisitely timed; the interval of pause might have been clocked a hundred times without the variation of a hundredth of a second; the throw drew easily forward, shooting the fly far and true to the full length of the line where it hovered motionless an instant, and then settled to the water like a feather upon a casual breeze or like one of the winged seeds that sometimes drift down upon the stream. There was not the semblance of a jerk, not the minutest interruption of this oiled routine. . . .

Our eyes were fixed upon the all-unconscious exhibition—for he was completely unaware of an audience—and something akin to a hypnotic spell fastened on us there in that heat and stillness of the noon. It was scarcely believable, such casting, and yet we were looking at it. I began to realize, as he came closer, that here was the product of many influences: of inborn genius, of years and years of application, and of something yet more—the high devotion of the artist to his art. I could see his face now, and it had upon it the pure, quiet light of elation. It was not quite smiling, but it was supremely and deeply happy with the rare happiness of mastery. I watched his face, relieved thus to divert my close attention from the intolerable perfection of his casting, and saw it to be deep-scored with life and stained with the pigments of almost a century's weathers. The expression did not change: It was as constant as the backward and forward rhythm of his arm and body. Indeed, it was more constant, for it was still in its eternal mold after something had broken at last the iteration of that physical routine. . . .

For now, for the first time since he had rounded that lower bend, one of his forward casts did not come back.

In this protracted spell of admiration and wonder I had forgotten that the old man was actually fishing for trout. He had not forgotten it, however, nor forgotten what to do in the event of the present contingency. For he had struck and hooked what appeared to be a heavy, deep-fighting native while I had been intent upon his face. That super-alertness without which no trout can be hooked on a dry fly had been there all the time, ready and waiting. The impeccable mechanics of his casting had not disturbed this nice adjustment, this essentially human equilibrium of nerves.

But now in the higher tension, in the electric air of the battle, it seemed that the machine was again dominant after its deference to the purely human interim. Here was merely another functioning of the machine: playing a trout differed from casting a fly only as the action of a motor in high gear differed from its action in low. Both were faultless, synchronized, delicately right.

I remember how that trout went away, sounding for the rocky caverns of the west bank. The water was deep in there, black under its surface of slow suds, a broad eddy backing from the main current. *Salvelinus* had allies, no doubt, in this submarine grotto: roots and rocks and the sunken lit-

ter that piles in every deep, still pocket of a stream. Freedom was there if he could reach it with a yard or two of not overly taut line. But the old man knew it as well, and he was keeping *Salvelinus* off. Coaxing him away, as it were. What impressed mc throughout that struggle was the gentleness of it and the absence of haste. Watching it, I had at no time the feeling that tackle was being strained. The old man steered that boring fish away from the haven he sought in the deep eddy, back into the central shallows, and across to a clear run of water over the sandy bottom of the east side. The fish turned downstream now, racing fast with the current and gaining slack. I held my breath. But there was a marvelously efficient stripping in of line—a left-handed operation so casual and unhurried as to be almost contemptuous, and yet so effective that the trout came abreast of the old man on a line that held only inches of slack and went past, downstream, against pressure again.

My heart may have missed a beat or two at this juncture of the battle as I thought, for the first time, of that five-foot staff. I had come to accept that thing subconsciously—it had been so easily handled, so definitely unobtrusive in all the exercise of casting and of playing the fish—but now I realized that some sort of shift must be made as the old gentleman turned to face the battle downstream. The stick had been wedged into his right armpit, sloping away a little behind him and braced against a convenient rock to hold his slight figure in the current. . . . This, I felt, would be a maneuver delicate in the extreme and not without an element of real danger.

But while I deliberated about offering assistance the thing was done. It was disappointingly easy—in fact, no maneuver at all, but a mere pivoting of his body in a semi-circle, using the staff as a sort of axis for the turn without moving its lower end in the slightest, so that now he had his prop before him instead of behind. It looked easier that way and the thought occurred to me that, far from being concerned at the necessity of turning, he was actually

relieved by it and glad of the opportunity! The whole affair was of a piece with all the rest of his stream technique—so bewildering in its facility that I began to think he must have some elemental affinity with the water itself.

———

The fight wore along, drew itself out to an exorbitant length, verged almost upon boredom. That trout had every fair chance to escape that any fighting trout can have and yet it had no chance. It was simply unlucky in having taken the fly of a master. That gentle, inexorable pressure wore it down, turned it again and again on the apparent edge of escape. There was a growing feebleness in its rushes, and I knew now that only one result was possible. I almost turned away—but there was still the matter of landing, the matter of handling rod, net, and staff with two arms. . . . The old chap would drown him, perhaps, in the swift water, when the fish was completely exhausted, and thus obviate the necessity of the net.

But no; he was bringing the trout in, now, but not up through the central channel. *Salvelinus* had worked over to the eastern shore and from there the old gentleman brought him home, yard by yard, a cross-current job through quiet water. No thought of drowning there. With ten feet of line still off the end of his rod the old-timer picked up his staff in his left hand, waded slowly to the shallow east shore, tossed the staff upon the bank, took the net with his now free left hand, drew the unresisting fish over it and lifted him clear.

Seventeen or eighteen inches, I guessed. I could see the orange underbody gleam in the sun. A beautiful fish, a prize in any trout water in the world.

I looked at Mill and he looked at me, and although we didn't speak I knew him to be thinking as I was, that the thing had been too perfect, too utterly lacking in any element of uncertainty. But a surprise was in store for us. The old man put the rod under his arm, stooped, and wet each hand in the stream, one at a time, shifting the net from one hand to the other. Then, with the net held under the other arm he grasped the trout in its meshes, released the fly from its mouth, and returned it very tenderly to the water. A slow ripple spread away toward midstream and disappeared. His extreme gentleness throughout the struggle was clear to us all at once.

He looked up, then, saw us, and smiled. "I have kept enough of them," he said, "in sixty-nine years."

"That would make him close to eighty," Mill remarked some time afterward, "if he started when he was about ten."

He paused to change his fly and entered the stream again with the indispensable staff. The casting recommenced, caught up the accustomed rhythm—the machine was again in low gear, the hand of the watch drew away from the hour. He went ahead upstream, inching his way, his slight, brown-clad figure breasting the current, diminishing slowly in the heat shimmer of that noontime until it was gone at last around the far bend. There seemed something symbolic in that inexorable creeping progression, as if he embodied those ultimate forces which nothing can stay, like the force of truth or the cosmic forces which keep the world on the move. That steady, slow headway would stop when the stream stopped, not before; it would cease when the banks closed in upon him in the far upper rills, when there was at last no water ahead for him to aim his fly at. Unless . . .

He didn't look his eighty years or more; he had the timeless quality of vigorous old age, the look of extended youth often seen on the faces of old men who have preserved some boy thoughts, particularly boy thoughts upon nature, the purest of all thoughts of boys or men. One could understand something of his fishing philosophy. Each bend of the stream, opening a new vista, was an extension of life for him. Up to the point which marked the next turn, here was a new experience waiting, a problem for the mind and body. He was in a sense deathless—proof, even, against decline—so long as he could hold that interest in the next ten minutes, so long as there was another bend to go around.

But some day, and it was not far off, there would be the last bend, the last problem of water, rocks, wind, and sun. And his own errorless mechanics would meet him then face to face, the perfect functioning of physical law.

APRIL 1935

HAROLD P. SHELDON—the Colonel, as I knew him—is best remembered for his masterful *Tranquility Trilogy* and his dedicated work in the field of conservation. He served as guns and shooting editor at *The Sportsman* in its later years, but he was equally well versed in the field of fly-fishing, as is proved here.

AN EXPERT OPINION

---

by HAROLD P. SHELDON

I SAY IT in sorrow," said Colonel Cushing, "but I believe the society of fishermen sustains more bubble reputations, more plausible quackery and a greater number of didactical know-it-alls than any other sport—with the possible exception of amateur horse racing. Eighteen years ago this same month of June, a fishing acquaintance whom I met at the Cast and Creel on the Battenkill gave me a dozen flies." He paused and from a pocket of his short-skirted fishing jacket produced a gigantic fly book.

This fly book, as such intimate articles are apt to be, was a measure of the man who used it. Someone—some ancient, patient craftsman, bespectacled and aproned—had selected the leather for it, a rich, tough piece, fine-fibered and not too flexible. He had then cut with skill and stitched with

patience, waxing his whips well so that now, after nearly twenty years of service, the sides gleamed with a dull polish undimmed by time or immersion; no stitch was frayed, no seam gaped open under the strain of encompassing some ten or twelve dozen assorted flies, as well as several hundred feet of leaders. In short, the material of this magnificent fly book, the fine, strong stitching and molding of the indomitable leather and most of all, perhaps, the tremendous size of the object all indicated that the old craftsman had a specially qualified patron in mind when he worked. Clearly, it was no book for the careless amateur trout fisherman; obviously, it was no book for the pleasant dabbler who fishes in order to be fashionable; and certainly, it was no book for the cautious person who fears to shove his shins into a deep riffle of cold water or who stays at home on a quiet gray day when the streams are running free and clear, because of the perils of black flies and mosquitoes. It was definitely and most particularly a book for a youngster of eighteen or so—as was the Colonel, in fact, when he bought it—who already anticipates that trout fishing is to be the major serious pastime of a long life and who enters upon the sport with diligence and a proper respect for its traditions and its obligations, wisely desiring his equipment to be in keeping. Two flies the Colonel extracted from the book and laid in his palm for better inspection.

"Only these remain of the original dozen," he resumed. "The gentleman didn't know the name, or possibly I neglected to ask. For all that I know, it may be something as common elsewhere as a Gray Hackle and unfamiliar only on these local streams, or it may be the creation of a specialist, never listed anywhere and only tied in a few dozens. I might have looked it up myself, of course, but after embarrassing a few experts, I became interested to see if any of these nomenclature purists could put a name to it. In eighteen years none has done so." He fixed the Captain with a quizzical eye. "And now, my boy, it's your turn to try it. Your reputation has spread to every stream in New England. Let me see if you've earned it."

The third member of the party, the Doctor, set the butt of his rod on the sod and watched the Colonel and the Captain. Behind them in the Pond a trout took down a floating insect with a brief sucking noise and a wide, silent roll of water.

The Captain gave the flies a sharp inspection.

"Soldier Palmer," said he, in tones of secure authority, his gaze meeting the other's glance fairly. "It's funny no one has named it for you long before this."

The tableau held for a moment, and then on the green bank of the Trout Pond, with the declining sun sprinkling the participants with reflections of its own passing glory, the Colonel bent his long back in a quaintly deferential bow to the expert.

"The only man in eighteen years who really knew," he murmured.

"Well, gentlemen, the trout are rising," said the Doctor, an observation that was repeatedly confirmed by the countless splashes on the water where the six- and eight-inch fish were feeding with more vigor than finesse and by the occasional deep, slow roll where some venerable trout picked off an insect with the lazy, easy, dignified form that marks the veteran whose perfect timing, as well as whose knowledge of his own supremacy, makes rude haste unnecessary and spattering drops the sign of vulgar competition.

"Colonel, as the honored guest of the Squaretail Club, you are to choose the water you like most to fish. There's the Pond and nearly four miles of good stream, so you need feel no hesitancy in making your selection."

"Well, now, that's right nice of you boys. If it's agreeable to all, I believe I'll just take the left shore of the Pond and cast from the bank. I observe certain matters and things that seem to indicate that some notable fish are feeding just off shore. I shall fish well ahead and keep my shadow off the water."

"When you reach the point, sir, lay your cast just inside an old stake you'll see in the cove—there's a black behemoth who feeds there, and he'll run close to four pounds, I reckon," the Captain advised, as the guest moved up the bank, working out his line with smooth, slow flicks of his wrist. "Where'll we go, Doctor?"

"Why, on an evening like this we could take fish in the middle of the meadow! Look at that one roll! Let's take the skiff and drift up the channel."

They had been quietly at work for perhaps a quarter of an hour when a whoop from the Colonel—a person not normally inclined to emotional vociferation—drew

From a sketch by
Ralph L. Boyer

their quick attention. That worthy fisherman was surging about in water nearly to his waist, grunting, gasping and occasionally letting go a frantic bawl of pure excitement. His rod was weaving and whipping like a rush in a gale, and farther out, just where the edge of the alder shadows fell on the darkling water, the erstwhile placid surface heaved and boiled and was cut athwart by slashing passages of the line. No fin showed; the struggle was deep, strong and furious.

"He's fast to one of the Old Masters!" exclaimed the Captain. Now and again on the Squaretail waters someone struck a fish of such extraordinary weight and of such unusual coloring that it was supposed to be an original denizen of the stream or a direct descendant of such. The ordinary run of fish were dark enough, in all conscience, but these ancients were a glossy black, in certain lights, showing the barely perceptible greenish tint of jade. Against their somber sides, the crimson spots glowed like sparks. Truly, they were fish to make one weep for the olden days, were these Old Masters; and their strength, prudence and utter, unrelenting courage were such that, while thousands of their lesser kind went from fly to creel and from creel to the pan on the hot griddle of the battered stove in the cabin, these superior fish were seldom struck and much more rarely taken.

The two in the skiff watched the strug-gle with bated breath, and a black duck with her brood swam to the edge of the rushes and watched too. The angler was fully alive to his tremendous opportunity, and for all his thrashing and whooping, he fought a neat, tight battle, keeping the opponent's flanking rushes well under control and holding a perilous reserve of line under his hand. A raft of water-lilies floated near the farther fringe of the conflict.

"If he ever makes the pads, he's gone!" said the Doctor, but time and time again the rod whipped up in a straining arc just in the instant to turn the fish from the haven. At times, his jetty snout and gaping jaws must have missed the swaying stems by inches only. But as direct rushes failed to carry him through against the supple resistance of rod and wrist, the Old Master attempted his goal by a series of tacking rushes, opposing cunningly the broad width of his side against the rod; but this maneuver, which might have won for him had he adopted it while his strength was fresh, failed him now, and though he strained every sinew and fought until the pads bobbed and quivered in the currents created, he just missed getting his nose into the saving tangle. Three minutes later, the Colonel lifted the expiring warrior in his net and prudently lugged his fish some twenty yards into the meadow before lifting the prize for the inspection of the Doctor and the Captain in the skiff.

"What did he take?" called one of the two, after admiring and congratulatory messages had been shouted back and forth.

"Soldier Palmer!" was the reply, "and he ruined it—stripped it to the bare shank!"

The Doctor gazed searchingly at his friend.

"That reminds me," said he in lower tones, "what was that fly?"

"Hanged if I know," was the bland response. "Never saw one of 'em before in my life."

"Aha! I thought so! You charlatan! You shyster! Why, the cold-blooded effrontery of it! And to the Colonel, too, who ranks you a mile and who can spot a liar just by looking at him. I can't but admire such bold, uncompromising duplicity!"

"Well, you see," the other began mildly, "he challenged me, didn't he, to name that fly? Why the devil didn't he name it himself if he's so good at it? Was he risking his reputation? Not so you could notice it, but he compelled me to risk mine, and I took him at his own game. You ought to be proud of me!"

"I am," admitted his crony, "but I'm also worried over what he'll think of you if ever he finds out what that fly really is!"

"Well, that's a chance I had to take, of course. But he hasn't found out in eighteen years, has he? Besides, he's only got one of 'em left now—that Old Master has just ruined one. If he only loses the other, I'll be safe, for you can't hold a man to a description of a trout fly from memory. We've got all the fish we need, haven't we? Let's go on."

An hour later, with the twilight fading, the Colonel far up the shore regretfully reeled in his line and untied his cast. Groping about in the gloom of the alders, he got hold of his heavy creel and set out toward the cabin, following the drift of a fragrance that seemed to be an agreeable blend of frying trout, boiling coffee and browning corn bread.

"What luck?" chorused the two from the kitchen as the late fisherman stumbled up the steps into the light.

"I only saved two," was the reply, given in tones of quiet restraint, as the speaker laid, not one, but two genuine and authentic Old Masters on the dining-room table. For the space of a minute no one spoke and the great dark fish reposed there on the dark walnut with the yellow light gleaming on their ebony magnificence, their crimson spots glowing like coals.

"Great Scott!" said the Doctor and the Captain, and it was inadequate.

"I saved but the two," repeated the Colonel in low, dramatic tones, "and they cost me the last of my Soldier Palmers given me so long ago at the Cast and Creel on the Battenkill. But they are worth it."

Still later, when their old friend had feasted and departed with his two fish, the

Doctor laid aside his pipe, rose and from a shelf over the lounge took down a massive tome devoted, from cover to cover, to matters pertaining solely to the noble art of fly-fishing for trout. It was a big, authentic-looking book. Turning the pages, he came to a section filled with carefully executed, exquisitely colored illustrations of trout flies. After examining some scores of these reproductions, he paused with a finger on the page to indicate a certain specimen but held it so that the name could not be read.

"What is it?" he demanded, as the other leaned forward to look. There it was—the perfect picture of the lost flies of the Battenkill.

"I swear I don't know," faltered the guilty rascal as the Doctor fixed him with an unwavering eye.

Whereupon the inquisitor moved his finger a half inch down the page, so that the delicately etched wording could be read.

———

(Author's Note.) Being cognizant of the ancient, cruel suspicion with which the public regards the strange coincidences of the fisherman's life, I find myself reluctant to write the conclusion of this wholly veracious narrative. As between anglers, will you, yourself, then have one guess as to the name of the particular trout fly that our friend the Doctor found in the big, authentic-looking book?

JUNE 1936

THE ARTISTS

RALPH BOYER'S many contributions to sporting art were topped by his work for Eugene Connett's Derrydale Press, which published ten of his prints and etchings. E. Phillips Williamson, who knows perhaps more about Derrydale than anyone else, rates Boyer's work among the very finest of the Derrydale output.

AIDEN LASSELL RIPLEY needs no introduction to readers, for his work ran the gamut from fine art to etchings and pen and pencil sketches such as those seen here. Old-time *Field & Stream* readers will remember his *Gunning in America* prints, and collectors cherish his work.

ACKNOWLEDGMENTS

THIS IS not my book. My only function is to bring you the work of others. Were it not for Powell Cabot, Richard Danielson, and Christian Herter and their outstanding magazine, there would be no words, and without the enthusiastic support of my editor, Laura Jorstad, and The Countryman Press, there would be no book. I am in their debt. I am also indebted to Ken Callahan for his enlightened introduction and to Col. Henry A. Siegel and John T. Ordeman for their knowledge and assistance.

All too often a volume such as this is compiled without considering the possible conflicts of copyrights. Not so here. Every effort has been expended to contact the heirs of these long-ago contributors to *The Sportsman*; in instances where this proved impossible, each article was researched at the Library of Congress and found to be—as I had expected—in the public domain. I am indebted to the children, grandchildren, and heirs apparent of Ralph Boyer, Frederick White, Eugene Connett III, Samuel G. Camp, John Alden Knight Jr., Henry M. Hall, Edward R. Hewitt, Preston J. Jennings, Howard T. Walden II, and Harold P. Sheldon for both their permission and their enthusiasm; and to Rita Maturi and the staff at the Library of Congress for their assistance in the search for nonexistent copyright renewals. To each and all, my sincere thanks. Special thanks go to my father for being a part of both *The Sportsman* and my life, and to my five children for their continued support.

—RALF COYKENDALL
Manchester Center, Vermont